COLIN POWELL AND THE AMERICAN DREAM

COLIN POWELL AND THE AMERICAN DREAM

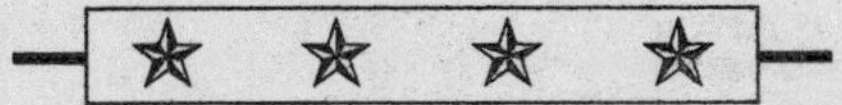

Judith Cummings
and Stefan Rudnicki

Preface by Roy Innis
National Chairman, Congress of Racial Equality

Conclusion by Jeanne V. Bell

ISBN 0-7871-0936-3

Printed in the United States of America

Dove Books
301 North Cañon Drive
Beverly Hills, CA 90210

Distributed by Penguin USA

Text design and layout by Stanley S. Drate/
Folio Graphics Co., Inc.
Cover design and layout by Bear Canyon Creative
Cover photograph courtesy of AP/Mike Fisher

First Printing: November 1995

10 9 8 7 6 5 4 3 2 1

ACKNOWLEDGMENTS

The logistics of writing this book meant that quite a number of pieces of an otherwise disorganized world had to fall into place very quickly . . . entropy reversed. For their roles in this process, we thank contributors Roy Innis and Jeanne V. Bell; Patricia J. MacKay and Francis Rivera of the Entertainment Technology Communications Group; Marcia Gottsegen and Joy Claussen; all those at Dove who instantly rallied to the project with their valuable assistance: Mary Aarons, Lara Alameh, Chris Hemesath, Margaret Maldonado, Julie McCarron, Rick Penn-Kraus, Paul Pirner, Michele Samet . . . and Michael Viner.

COLIN POWELL, HAMLET OF HARLEM, THE SPHINX OF THE PENTAGON, OR THE EISENHOWER OF THE 90's?

---

by
Roy Innis

Who is Colin Powell? Is he Hamlet, Sphinx, or Eisenhower? The answer is simple; he is all of the above.

For the remainder of this century, and well into the next—and possibly beyond that—volumes will be written about General Powell in an attempt to more accurately define his essence. This book about Colin Powell by Judith Cummings and Stefan Rudnicki—following the General's own very successful autobiography—is probably the first of a long list to follow.

Preface

Powell mania is an undeniable political phenomenon. It is reminiscent of the earlier political mania that developed in our country around George Washington, Andrew Jackson, Ulysses Grant, and Dwight Eisenhower. Before running for the presidency, these soldiers, like Colin Powell, were popular and successful generals. But it is the personality, style, and historical proximity of General Eisenhower that most parallels that of General Powell.

Powell, like Eisenhower, was born into a family of hardworking people of modest means. Both were fortunate to gain entrance into especially good schools: Powell attended the old City College of New York (CCNY); while Eisenhower attended the United States military academy (West Point).

Powell and Eisenhower were not especially good students in academic subjects, but they excelled in the military arts. They adapted rapidly to military life as young lieutenants and were noticed early in their careers by powerful people in the military establishment. Their industrious performance of duty earned them promotions and key assignments within the army, and special assignments serving Washington,

DC, political and military elites. Both men in their eras achieved the highest rank in their profession, and at the end of their distinguished military careers were called upon to perform new duties as civilians.

In stressful, critical times, nations tend to look to successful, popular military men for leadership. It is assumed by many that successful leadership on the battlefield can be transferred wholesale to civilian institutions. And, although history has not borne out that belief, many people still hold on to that notion.

Of the generals mentioned, who became President, only Andrew Jackson carried a strong, assertive leadership style into the White House. "Ike" did not. Even in the military, that was not his style.

While there are tremendous similarities in the military careers and the leadership styles of General Eisenhower and General Powell, one should not conclude that Powell will necessarily maintain a moderately low-key leadership style as a president. Despite Powell's and Eisenhower's similarities, there is one big difference: Powell is a black man.

If Powell becomes President of the United

States of America, he would be the first of his race to have that ultimate responsibility. In this way, Powell's situation would be more like that of Andrew Jackson's, when he won the presidency in 1828, than like that of Dwight Eisenhower, when he became president in 1952.

Andy Jackson (Old Hickory) was the first of his social class to achieve that height in the young nation. Jackson was a backwoodsman, a common man; he came neither from the class of the planter aristocrats nor from the class of the commercial and financial elites as did the six previous presidents. Jackson had to be tough and aggressive, the "Tribune of the people," or he would have been devoured by the elites.

Eisenhower, although a commoner by birth, was not the first of his class to achieve the presidency. "Ike" had the luxury to be a benign, amiable grandfather.

Colin Powell's Hamlet-like quality—hesitating at almost each step as he climbed up the ladder of success—has been, so far, an effective device for him. Similarly, his Sphinx-like persona—silent but apparently powerful—has served him well. His Eisenhower-type image has served him well also.

Ordinarily, despite his race, these qualities would have been enough for him to win a major party nomination and, eventually, the presidency of the United States. But recent developments in race relations in America have seriously disturbed this calculus.

As the country was trying to recover from the pain caused by the brutal assault on Rodney King by racist officers of the Los Angeles police department, a series of other atrocities ensued. Some of these atrocities were the racist verdict of an almost all-white jury in suburban Simi Valley that "cut loose" the brutal police officers; the riots by minorities in South Central Los Angeles; the brutal racist beating of Reginald Denny, a white man, by Damien Williams and Henry Watson, two black hoodlums; and the racism of the overwhelmingly black jury that, in effect, cut them loose, convicting them of only minor charges.

Before, during, and after these racially-based atrocities emanating from the Los Angeles area, similar ones were occurring in other parts of the country—especially in the New York City area. Black demonstrators, bootlegging under the banner of "civil rights," conducted an illegal, racist boycott against some Korean-owned stores in the Flatbush section of Brooklyn, New York.

The first black mayor of New York City, David Dinkins, and then the city's second black Commissioner of Police, Lee Brown, did not enforce an injunction ordering the racist boycotters to cease and desist all illegal activities in front of the Korean-owned stores, even when the order issued by New York Supreme Court was sustained upon appeal.

Those very senior black political leaders enforced the court-issued injunction only after I—as the National Chairman of the Congress of Racial Equality—filed a class-action federal civil rights suit against them. These officials, ordinarily good men, were sued for violating the civil rights of both the Korean store-owners and over 100 black and Latino senior citizens and mothers who wanted to continue shopping in those stores. As a civil rights leader for a quarter of a century and a veteran of over three decades as a tireless warrior for all humanity, this was a painful and embarrassing chore.

Racists, even black racists, actively involved in immoral lawlessness had to be confronted. Black officials who passively or actively acquiesce with racist, immoral lawlessness must be challenged. Dare we not do exactly to black racists that which we did when we challenged white racism at the height of our nation's great racial equality awakening?

After the so-called Korean boycott was defeated, some of the racist participants sparked and took part in a riot that turned into a virtual pogrom against Jews and many decent black people in the Crown Heights section of Brooklyn, New York. In one of those nights of horror, a young Jewish seminary student, Yankel Rosenbaum, was stabbed to death by a young black hoodlum.

Once again there was willing inaction, almost paralysis, on the part of New York City's black officials. Compounding this madness, an overwhelmingly black jury "cut loose" the young black assailant, ignoring palpable evidence, while accepting special allegations of white racism and police misconduct by planting of evidence.

These incidents, and numerous others (both real and imagined offenses) committed by both blacks and whites against their racial opposites have created an increasingly racially-charged environment all over America.

Into this atmosphere, the "mother of all trials," the O.J. Simpson trial occurred. For over a year, it was the most divisive issue in America, and became even more so when the verdict of not guilty was announced by a jury that was 75% black, over 80% minority.

Soon thereafter, with hardly any time for racial healing, America was confronted with the "father of all marches," the much-vaunted Louis Farrakhan "Million's Man March"—for black men only.

This is the environment that makes General Powell's quest for the presidency different than any of the other generals who succeeded to that great office.

And if Powell should be successful in that quest, he would have to adopt or develop a leadership style far different than any we have seen from him or from any of the other generals/politicians before them.

In this book, the reader must look carefully for signs that Colin Powell has that potential.

—Roy Innis

November 11, 1995

1

> Throughout the inhabited world, in all times and under every circumstance, the myths of man have flourished; and they have been the living inspiration of whatever else may have appeared out of the activities of the human body and mind. Myth is the secret opening through which the inexhaustible energies of the cosmos pour into human cultural manifestations.
>
> —JOSEPH CAMPBELL
> *The Hero with a Thousand Faces*

It has been decades since the last American hero.

Dynasties have fallen.

Celebrities with dubious credentials have popped into the glare of public attention, only to fade back into relative anonymity after their moment passed. When was the last time the word "hero" could be used without a hint of irony or embarrassment?

That General Colin Luther Powell can comfortably command that title is a sign of the man's unique qualifications and of the times into which he has emerged.

No one is a hero in private. Derived originally from the Greek, the word has connotations of courage, service, and self-sacrifice. A hero is a guardian, a protector. He is someone we trust. Without a constituency, without a people to protect and serve, there is no hero. Without public recognition there is no hero. It is the public's perception that makes it so. And there has to be an event, some opportunity, to ignite that hero's light for all to see.

For General Powell, a long and highly distinguished career in the military was only the fuel. Operation Desert Shield and the perceived success of the Gulf War provided the Promethean spark.

What is it that makes a hero? Are heroes born or made? Are they required to have superhuman strength or powers? The ancient Greeks wrestled with these questions and handed down a legacy potentially as confusing as it is massive.

Homeric heroes were, above all, human. If Achilles was a master warrior, he was also subject to fits of jealousy. And, of course, he had that famous soft spot, his heel. Another prominent soldier, Philoctetes, derived his power from one thing only; he possessed the bow that would fire the arrow that would win the Trojan War. Otherwise, he was a generally unpleasant person with an incurable wound so offensive to others that he had to be quarantined on an island away from human habitation until summoned for the final moments of the war.

To the Greeks and, apparently, to all cultures, heroes are needed as models, examples, mirrors. It is their very humanity that allows us access to them and tells us that we too have the potential in us to be heroes. Lowly beginnings, serious adversity, even actual handicaps are part of hero lore. These are among the elements that make up the typical hero's journey. Psychologist C. G. Jung and popular mythologist Joseph Campbell are probably the most prominent modern thinkers who have studied and articulated the mythic patterns of that journey as they repeat themselves among literally hundreds of cultures and societies.

In life as in literature, consciously or not, we look for those patterns, and when we recognize them we know we are in the presence of a hero.

When Colin Powell describes himself as a "late bloomer," referring to his undistinguished early years, we hear that everyone can get a second chance, that there is opportunity for all, whatever their beginnings, to transcend. That he is black simply raises the stakes, suggesting to persons of all ethnic and religious backgrounds that virtually *anyone* can become a force to be reckoned with. In Powell's story of success we recognize an echo of the only minority that really counts, our own minority of one—the individual. And in some fundamental way, we are no longer alone.

There are undoubtedly people who, despite General Powell's recent wave of popularity, will not like him; because of his views on key issues, or by virtue of political bias, or simply because of his race. But no rational person can deny him the title of hero.

Colin Powell has a look about him that balances warmth with authority, teddy-bear gentleness with guarded privacy. That he is a warrior, with thirty-five years of military life, is no threat to us. It is rather a reassurance that he can be the protector and guardian for which we, his extended family, are so desperately searching.

And, after all, what better place for a hero to distinguish himself than in the military, an institution that still places a high premium on values like loyalty, discipline, and command structures in a world that has otherwise all but abandoned such traditions.

Family is very important to Powell. But his parents, wife, and children are not the only family in his life, and he often refers to the army as another family, one that took him in and taught him perhaps as much as his own parents. And beyond the military and even government, there is the suggestion of yet a larger extended family, characterized by a long list of national, transnational, and global concerns.

The word stewardship comes up again and again in Powell's interviews, placing an emphasis on responsibility and service to others, guardianship of a sort.

Even his curiously cross-cultural name, Colin Luther Powell, seems to define his purpose and being. Colin and Powell derive from Gaelic and Welsh names meaning "virile" and "attentive" respectively, while Luther is a variation on the Teutonic "Lothar" or "fighter." The resulting "manly, attentive fighter" could describe any number of archetypal heroes, not the least of whom would be General Powell himself.

It is sometimes said that heroes come into prominence when they are most needed. Certainly, timing is critical. Every four years, this country experiences a presidential campaign and election. The schedule is rigid, and conforms to no other natural or historical cycle. Every four years we open the door to the hero we await. Most of the time, he's just not there. The door swings shut after having allowed some lesser light, some smaller figure, into the inner sanctum.

The nation and the world are dissatisfied.

But now and then, just occasionally, there's a hero ready and able to cross that threshold and take full charge of the reigns of state. This could be such a time.

2

There is a tide in the affairs of men,
Which, taken at the flood, leads on to fortune . . .
On such a full sea are we now afloat,
And we must take the current when it serves,
Or lose our ventures.

—WILLIAM SHAKESPEARE
Julius Caesar

Colin Powell has been mostly immune to the kind of bashing the media give other wannabe statesmen. Even the usually skeptical *Rolling Stone* showed respect by recently running a subhead stating that "The Best Thing Colin Powell Could Do For the Nation is Run for President."

It could be his manner: gentlemanly, candid, and at times disarmingly funny.

Maybe it's because he has assiduously avoided any suggestion that he actually desires power, prestige, or presidency. This has its appeal since we are familiar with the wry epithet that any man who seeks the presidency can't be trusted with it. After all, Dwight D. Eisenhower, one of Powell's acknowledged ideals and role models, was virtually drafted into the presidency after repeatedly denying in public that he was even remotely interested in the job.

But maybe Powell's romance with the media has another source. Maybe they simply like him, or at least see in him someone they would like to like.

As the countdown to his announcement about running for the presidency approaches zero hour, there seems less and less said or written anywhere that could be construed as criticism. Instead, there is a palpable awareness that the man has the stature of a myth. With reference to the difficulty people have had learning his plans, he has been characterized as "the four-star Sphynx." Likewise, his ability to avoid direct answers to questions of political strategy has labeled him "Delphic," after the ancient Greek oracle at Delphi, known for its ambiguous and sometimes misleading prophecies. These are classical references of a sort rarely if ever used by today's undereducated and over-jargoned purveyors of information.

Powell's position with the media has not always been as positive. As recently as August 27, 1995, the *New York Times* ran an in-depth Sunday feature critical of, among other things, what has come to be called "the Powell Doctrine." This is the principle, maintained by General Powell, that "there should be no use of force unless success is all but guaranteed. Force should be used decisively and its application should preferably be short. As soon as the aims are achieved, American forces should be quickly extracted, lest the military fall into a quagmire." Among others, Eliot A. Cohen, a military specialist at Johns Hopkins University, damned General Powell with faint praise saying, "This is a guy who has been a very cautious upholder of the national security system. He is bright but has never made a bold decision on a public policy matter." Citing examples as diverse as the Gulf War, Bosnia, and the Somalia crisis, the article called the doctrine "an inadequate guide," suggesting that Powell's record has been weak and indecisive.

But the publication only days later of Powell's

monumental autobiography, *My American Journey*, and the subsequent book tour with its concomitant round of media interviews, seemed to put to rest any serious stirrings of negativity in the media.

Whatever their reasons, the media have been echoing a groundswell of popularity that has placed Powell ahead of President Clinton by a consistent ten percent margin over a period of several months. Except for anti-abortion pickets and the occasional vulgar heckler, like the one that made it through on the call-in segment of Powell's *Larry King Live* interview, his critics have remained at a distance; he has been protected, it seems, by a blanket of media approval.

It has been suggested that Powell's candidacy, should it materialize, will be characterized by personality rather than issues, and headlines such as *Newsweek*'s "CAN COLIN POWELL SAVE AMERICA?" and *U.S. News & World Report*'s "COLIN POWELL: SUPERSTAR" bear that out. Powell has certainly exhibited a reluctance to be tied to political issues, choosing instead to stand for only a few "core beliefs," leaving his position on numerous other matters vague or unknown.

"I'm not trying to put positions out to satisfy any particular part of the political spectrum," Powell says. "I'm just going to speak my mind as honestly as I can, and whatever that does to the polls, I don't care. I know that politics is also the art of compromise, but I have some core beliefs, and I'm not going to tack and change every time some criticism comes my way if there are core beliefs that I am defending."

The thrust of Powell's vision, bolstered by his life experience, is nothing if not clear.

First and foremost is his sense of family, both inner and extended. He sees America itself as, ultimately, a family. And it is a family with a manifest destiny reminiscent of the frontier spirit of the mid-nineteenth century. America, to Powell, has been established by "divine providence" to lead the world. With that belief come a host of other ancillary assumptions, not only about foreign policy, but also on other more personal matters like responsibility, education, and race. Words like "democratic" and "republic," when spoken by Powell, bear a classic dignity they have seldom had in this century. It is a comprehensive vision, and it transcends the artificial contructs and postures of merely political platforms. It is those "core beliefs" again. The issues are the man.

And the man appears to identify himself as a force for change, albeit a "centrist," someone forever seeking "the middle ground, where you can get most of the people thinking alike." He adds, "That is what constitutional democracy in America is all about." Consistent with the relatively apolitical slant of his life, Powell admits that he has never been registered as a voter with either the Republican or Democratic parties, but has voted independently.

According to Powell, "There is a revolution taking place in American politics, and in the politics of all the Western democracies."

That revolution is the result of the end of the cold war with the demise of the Soviet Union in 1991. "We don't have to worry about the godless Communists, the evil empire, the nuclear Armageddon any more," says Powell. "What shall we worry about? The answer is home. Violence. Crime. Drugs. Children not being educated. The breakdown of moral order in our society." Powell says that the revolution is continuing because neither President Bush nor President Clinton have been able to respond quickly or effectively enough to these domestic concerns. He feels that Americans are growing "more conservative" in the sense that they want less government in their lives. But the American people "are also known to speak inconsistently," so that they also do not want to lose what government provides for them. "We're in a fascinating period here, and it's going to be great fun to watch."

★ *Beginning with the domestic front, here are a few areas about which Colin Powell has made himself particularly clear.*

The family must be the first and final arbiter of basic human values, and the source of a moral education. In response to the loaded right-wing phrase, "family values," Powell condemns any imposition or legislation of values by one group over another, while reinforcing repeatedly the importance of family. He describes his own family, his model, as "good people, believing in this country, wanting a better life, and wanting to raise a family that would do better than they did. That's the American dream, the immigrant dream."

A firm believer in God and in prayer, Powell nevertheless believes that "prayer fundamentally belongs in the home and in the church," while a pledge of allegiance followed by a moment of silence might be appropriate to a school setting. He is profoundly opposed to rules that dictate how a prayer might be offered in school.

"The church," Powell says, "can play a very valuable role by teaching the difference between right and wrong, by teaching people to treasure other people. And frankly, the Ten Commandments is about the best value system you could come up with."

Powell insists that he is pro-choice, though not pro-abortion. He supports every woman's right to decide whether or not she is to have a child, and he says, "The law of the land says a woman has the right to make that choice." But he recommends alternatives such as adoption to abortion. "A child is a valuable creation," he has said.

He does not support government funding of abortions, seeking instead to find ways of making adoption easier.

The related issue of teen pregnancy leads Powell once again squarely back to the responsibility of the family and church to educate and set examples. He and his wife, Alma, support a local Washington group called "Best Friends" that goes into the inner city to counsel and educate young girls.

On Medicare, Powell supports the generally Republican line of controlling rising growth cost without necessarily cutting back on services, while on other family-related fiscal issues, he is quick to point out that all the evidence is not yet in. For example, setting a family cap on welfare may ultimately be hurtful to children, without necessarily discouraging the growth of large families among the poor.

Powell defends the right to bear arms. As a military man, he would naturally own weapons. But he also supports registration of weapons and reasonable investigation of would-be registrants.

When asked about environmental issues, Powell asserts that he is "a person who feels deeply about this country. God has given us this land, and we need to be good stewards of our land," so that we can "pass on to our children and grandchildren something of value." He cautions, however, that "we have to do it in such a way that it does not rob us of the use of these valuable assets . . . that can be used to produce jobs which people need."

Powell calls himself "a fiscal conservative" and "an unabashed capitalist" with "the greatest faith in the entrepreneurial system." He continues, "I feel that government should do everything possible to free the creative energy that exists in American industry. I like the creation of wealth. Very Republican. At the same time, while we're creating that wealth, government has the responsibility to make sure that all parts of our society are dealt with, that all of our common needs as a nation are dealt with. I am concerned that some of my *friends* in the political spectrum tend to overlook that. In their desire to cut government, to throw out the bureaucrats, to cut taxes, they may do it in a way that does not take into full consideration the needs of our fellow Americans who are desperate and who need help. So I am probabaly more liberal than the mainstream of the Republican party right now."

Focusing on taxes, Powell states that they "should be kept as low as possible. Nobody wants to see a tax burden higher than the one we have now, and if it's possible to reduce it, we should reduce it, but we have to do it in a way that shows we're good stewards of our future as well, and not in a way that allows the deficit to increase (so that) we put a tax burden on future generations."

Asked about raising the minimum wage, Powell states that he is "not clear right now whether that creates more jobs or loses jobs."

★ *On politics and government, Powell repeatedly refers to the ongoing revolution mentioned earlier.*

While recognizing that democracy is "a noisy business," Powell asserts that "the American people are tired of the harshness that exists in the public dialogue between the Democrats and Republicans. They are disappointed that in all of the partisan bickering, their (Congress's) work is not being done."

In government as in the military, General Powell places great emphasis on structure and discipline. Although an open critic of President Clinton's loose White House style ("quite different from the style I was used to and more comfortable with"), Powell is quick to point out that "the right model is whatever the president wants, whatever works for him. Just because it's harder for me, that's irrelevant."

"We may be a two-party system," says Powell, "but we're not necessarily a two-party nation. As I have traveled around the country, I have found more and more people, especially in the last year and a half, who are not claiming to be either Republicans or Democrats. They are representing something different. They are disappointed with both of the major parties, and they're looking for something different. I think Ross Perot touched a very responsive chord, and since 1992 when he touched it, it has not gone away. I see it everywhere I go."

☆ *Race is, of course, a complex issue that comes up again and again.*

General Powell actively deplores and condemns racism in any form, whether it comes from Mark Fuhrman or Minister Louis Farrakhan.

Powell has at times been criticized as never having been involved in the black man's struggle in America, rooted as he is in a gentler Jamaican culture, and having grown up in a melting pot community in the South Bronx. Even his entry into the military came at a time when that institution was in the forefront of racial equality. "I was blessed and privileged," Powell admits, "to be in an institution that was leading the country in change with respect to race relations." Powell suggests that somehow these circumstances give him an advantage by providing a perspective that is not mired in a race struggle. To him, racism is the other guy's problem. He does not want O.J. Simpson to become the ultimate metaphor for American race relations.

For Powell, Affirmative Action still has a role, but he is against quotas.

Recalling his first real brushes with racism in the South, Powell says that "It would have been self-defeating for me to have put these problems on my shoulders, and worn them as a chip on my shoulder, or a knapsack full of stones holding me back. One of the most self-defeating emotions you can have is to take somebody else's racism and make it your problem."

Powell speaks with pride about being black, insisting that he never for a moment forgets about his race. "I see it in the morning when I look in the mirror." Nor does he want others to forget that he is black. Admitting that he is "light-skinned," he still insists that culturally, and with his "kinky hair and flat nose," he is "black as the ace of spades."

Were he to run for president, however, Powell would like to be viewed as the best for the job.

"I hope we reach the point in our national life in the not too distant future where people would say first, 'This is somebody I could vote for, or support for this office or the other. And it's also good that he's black. It shows that we've come a certain way in our country,' and not just instantly see me through a black filter."

In race issues as in other contexts, Powell stresses the importance of the rebirth of the family in the black community as the primary solution to the problems that face that community today. He speaks about returning to strong family traditions, and breaking "the cycle of illegitimacy that is plaguing our communities." Citing a statistic that fifty percent of prison inmates are black, Powell bemoans the wasted human resource. "I think we have to fix our education system. I think we have to restore a sense of pride. We have to teach our young people, once again, self-restraint, separating out right from wrong. I don't think any single government program or any single politician can fix it. I think what has to happen is all of us, as Americans, turning back to those of our citizens who are in need, who have not benefited from the American dream, who have not shared in the wealth of this country, and start to bring them up. African-Americans have to start with ourselves, and not look outside of our communities or outside of our own culture for this. We have got to start teaching our children again the way we were taught, the way I was taught, to behave and to have a sense of pride."

☆ *On matters related to the military Powell frequently speaks with the first person plural "we."*

Powell feels that an open statement of sexual preference in the military would be a problem. "I know there are gays serving in the military, and serving well. We ask them to make an additional sacrifice beyond the other sacrifices you have to make in the military service. We ask them to keep their sexual orientation a private matter. Military society is unlike any other part of American society. We tell you who to room with. We tell you who you're going to sleep with, and in the confines of barracks life, ship life, and military academy life, we thought that the presence of open homosexuality stated as a preference would be difficult, considering that we have very, very young people in the military. It's always going to be there. In the last few years we've cleaned out all the old shibboleths about 'they're security risks.' That's just not the case any more. It's an issue of privacy." Powell insists that these views are shared by all the Joint Chiefs of Staff and all the commanders, chaplains, and NCOs of the armed forces around the world.

"A good soldier," Powell asserts, "is dedicated to the business, the profession of soldiering. [Someone] who is loyal, who is willing to serve his nation, who is willing to sacrifice for his nation, and who believes in his nation. He is tough mentally, tough physically, has courage—the courage of his convictions as well as physical courage."

On war, he has said, "Nobody in his right mind who has seen war, who has seen death and war, can like war or want war."

According to Powell, it will not be necessary to reinstate the draft. "The volunteer force works superbly." Instead, he advocates some form of community service as part of high school education, "something like national service, but part of the high school experience."

☆ *Even on issues relating to foreign policy, there is a sense in Powell's statements of community, almost of family, among nations and peoples.*

His tours of duty in Vietnam clearly had a profound effect on General Powell, but he denies being "haunted" by the experience. There is no question, however, that the "Powell Doctrine" of quick, assured attack and immediate withdrawal is in direct contrast to the way in which that war was fought. He insists that if such a conflict were to happen again in the future, it is essential "that our political leaders have thought it through, established clear objectives, and that we (the military leaders) candidly and in all honesty tell them what the military is able to do and not able to do. And if we go to war, let's go to war fully, and not try to do it on the cheap, not try to do it without inconveniencing the American people."

Powell considers it a top priority of US foreign policy "to keep the process of democratization and market reform going in the republics of the former Soviet Union, and especially in Russia. Russia remains a superpower because of its size, because of its potential, and I think the revolution that has occurred over the last several years is still tenuous, and I think one of our most important foreign policy objectives, if not our most important one, is to keep that process moving forward in Russia."

Cuba for General Powell is becoming "an irrelevant leftover of the cold war." He feels that we will soon have to modify our policy and recognize the nation in order "to get ready for the collapse of Castro."

General Powell hopes we are "on the verge of a breakthrough in Bosnia," but has in the past consistently stood against armed intervention.

US presence in Korea is to Powell a very important commitment that must be maintained. He has concerns about North Korea as one of the few remaining communist nations in the world. "It's failing," he says.

Responding to criticism that the Gulf War may have been cut short, before a final victory was accomplished, Powell stresses that the American people perceive it as a successful engagement. He acknowledges the role of that conflict in bringing him to prominence. He speaks of "some lingering problems that are annoying, but not strategically important." His statement launching Operation Desert Storm has become famous, "Our strategy for going after this army is very, very simple. First we are going to cut it off, and then we are going to kill it."

3

There is a saying among soldiers:
I dare not make the first move but would rather play the guest.
I dare not advance an inch but would rather withdraw a foot.

This is called marching without appearing to move,
Rolling up your sleeves without showing your arm,
Capturing the enemy without attacking,
Being armed without weapons.

—LAO TSU
Tao Te Ching

"What does Colin Powell want to be, or not to be?—that is the question," asks the introductory line of an August 26, 1995 article from *The Times* of London.

Sometimes the clearest views of American social and political realities come from abroad, and this article continues by cogently presenting Powell's options. "He could run for president as an independent, found a third party, and utterly transform the shape of American politics. Or he could agree to stand as the running-mate to whichever Republican candidate is finally nominated, thus virtually assuring their election. Or he could wait, and run as a Republican or Democrat in the year 2000. Or he could live out the rest of his days on the lucrative lecture circuit at $60,000 a pop, a beloved national icon resting on his laurels."

That last option does not seem to be in Powell's vocabulary. He has said, "I want to do something that serves the nation. I have a passion for this country. I have a passion for contributing in some way, serving this country in some way. I just don't know if politics is the best way for me." He wants to "help Americans get together again, to somehow convey a message of hope into those parts of our American community where people are starting to lose hope. Let's start thinking of one another as a family. No successful part of the family can be satisfied with their success if there are other parts of the American family that are suffering and in need."

Refusing to be pinned down about a presidential run, he nevertheless expressed some satisfaction that, "Whether I enter the fray as a card-carrying, dues-paying, down-in-the-mud politician [or not], the national political debate has been widened, broadened." There seems little question that Powell wants to be a major force. He also wants to take advantage of his current popularity and the special position he currently enjoys. This does not seem to be a man who is likely to wait four more years before declaring candidacy.

He has also stated that he has "little interest in the vice presidency."

As to the mechanics of a potential candidacy, Powell, while not dismissing the possibility of running as a third-party or independent candidate, has used quasi-military language. "The route that makes the most tactical and technical sense is doing it as a Republican." Clearly among his many concerns must be the sixty million dollars that will come from the government to each of the two established parties, money he would have to raise independently if not associated with either. There is also the question, if elected, of governing the country independently, without the support of a certain number of committed members of Congress, literally having to start from scratch on every issue.

Powell believes that America is ready for a black president. "We really are at a point in our national life where we have progressed so far that it is possible for a black person to become President of the United States."

Why all the hesitation, then? "I have not spent my whole adult life trying to reach the point where I could run for elected political office. My whole life was spent in an entirely different direction, an entirely different profession, field—as a soldier." This fall's five-week book tour has been his opportunity to place his ideas before the people and to live under general scrutiny in a way perhaps comparable to public life. "I will have to see whether or not I really have something to contribute that is unique and different from everyone else, and whether I have the passion to pursue that vision, and I don't know that yet," he still says.

One of the major obstacles to Powell's candidacy is his family, who are described as having "little enthusiasm for that kind of exposure. Alma would prefer," he states, "that we remain a private couple, and not in elected public life. We have been a team for thirty-three years. We're a very close family. And it's a decision we would have to arrive at together."

As an October 2, 1995 *People* article put it, "If he decides to run for the White House, Powell's time of cozy domesticity—romping with his two grandsons, picking up "Styrofoam food" for lunch at the deli in the local Safeway, tinkering with his ancient Volvo—will be a thing of the past."

About other possibilities, he has said, "There are a range of options available to me, and if I decide not to seek the highest office in the land or enter elected politics, I will look at that entire range."

As an already quoted London *Times* article stated, "As an expert tactician, Powell will make no move until he is sure of sufficient support, but while he may be waiting for greatness to be thrust upon him, as one former Pentagon colleague observed: 'Make no mistake, Colin wants to be President—if not now, then later.' "

But does later really seem a viable option? Colin Powell's place is here, and his time is now. And he knows it. These opportunities will not come again. He knows that too. This is a man conscious of his standing in the world, his popularity. His military training has no doubt familiarized him with the essence of being a hero. A hero is there for his time and his people. He does not turn down an opportunity to be what he is—a hero. A presidential campaign in 1996 seems his most likely choice, but by no means his only choice.

In at least one interview, General Powell referred to the presidency *as one of* the most important positions in the nation, suggesting that there are others of perhaps equal weight. Whatever he chooses to do, there is little doubt he will be well prepared, and chances are good that he will achieve it.

And when did this preparation really begin?

Powell's childhood, as suggested before, was remarkably unremarkable, virtually unconscious. When does the hero's journey actually begin?

It's a contextual matter, really. The consciousness comes later, but the journey begins very early on. The signs are there: the obstacles, the call to adventure, the mentors, the synchronicities and accidents of fate that will not take "no" for an answer.

4

> Mine is the story of a black kid of no early promise from an immigrant family of limited means who was raised in the South Bronx . . .
>
> —COLIN POWELL
> *My American Journey*

The story begins, for Colin Luther Powell, on April 5, 1937, when he was born to a family living on Morningside Heights in Harlem. His sister, Marilyn, had been born five-and-a-half years earlier. Colin was the second child, the first son, of Maud Ariel ("Arie") McKoy Powell and Luther Theophilus Powell.

Luther Powell was born on the Caribbean island of Jamaica in 1898, the second of nine children, and emigrated to the United States in 1925 on a banana boat, a United Fruit Company steamer. He worked as a gardener on estates in

Connecticut and a building superintendent in Manhattan before going to work for a women's clothing manufacturer in New York's garment district, where he began in the stockroom, moved up to shipping clerk, and then became foreman of the shipping department.

Maud Ariel McKoy was the eldest of nine children and had the opportunity to complete high school and work for a time as a stenographer in a lawyer's office before leaving her native Jamaica. Maud's mother, Gram McKoy, had separated from Edwin McKoy, a sugar plantation overseer, and left Jamaica in search of work in Panama, then in Cuba, and then in the United States. There she found employment as a maid and a garment-district pieceworker, and she sent for her eldest child to help her. Maud had refused an earlier request to join her mother in Havana, which she had heard offered little in the way of opportunity. The prospect of low wages, long hours, and having to learn Spanish fueled Maud's refusal. She would join her mother only if Gram would move to New York City. Gram acquiesced, and in 1926, Maud, or Arie as she was known, arrived in New York City, in search of a brighter future.

To supplement her earnings, which she used chiefly to support her children still in Jamaica, Gram McKoy took in relatives and Jamaican immigrants as boarders in her Harlem apartment. One of these was Luther Powell, who met and courted Arie there. While they were engaged, both Luther and Arie were working in the garment district of Manhattan.

The marriage of Luther and Arie, on December 28, 1929, two months after the October stock market crash, united the Powell and McKoy bloodlines which, as is common in Jamaican heritage, included African, English, Irish, Scottish, and probably Arawak Indian, with the addition, on the Powell side, of a Jewish strain from a Broomfield ancestor.

The Powells were part of a proud, ambitious group of West Indians who worked hard to become financially secure and independent. A serious people with a dream of a better life, they believed wholeheartedly that the key to a better life was education and that success comes with hard work—"You must set a goal and do your job well," they told their children.

Some people set goals early on; they know what they want and they go after it. Others take more time. One interacts with one's surroundings, with awareness, without anxiety; the immediate circle widens gradually; in the larger field of experience, the goal emerges.

The time from birth to the identification of a goal is a grounding time. In heroic terms, it is the seed time, the preparation for the call to adventure.

5

Man follows the earth.

—LAO TSU
Tao Te Ching

Colin Luther Powell was born in the spring, the time of beginnings, born in 1937, a year of beginnings, many of which, like the man himself, got off to a slow start, but progressed steadily, finding their most effective forms or expression, realizing their great if originally unsuspected promise in the course of time.

In technology, which we say grows by leaps and bounds, the beginnings were often as undramatic as perhaps this particular birth, crucial, of course, to an immediate circle but in need of considerable development before emerging as operational, ready to work. Curiously, many are linked to the home; they were either invented in the kitchen or will wind up being used there. Others will link the home to the world beyond. And others will have still wider implications in the evolution of the modern world.

It is 1937.

The Miracle Mixer, soon renamed the Waring Blendor (with an "o"), is introduced at the National Restaurant Show in Chicago. Invented by Frederick J. Ossius, whose brother-in-law was band-leader Fred Waring's publicity director, the Blendor is sold primarily to bars to make frozen daiquiris. Not for another ten years, until 1947, will it be extensively promoted for home use.

Pharmacologist Daniele Bovet, working at the Pasteur Institute in France, develops the first antihistamine, but it will take another 13 years, until 1950, for antihistamines to become a popular remedy for colds and allergies, turning up in every home medicine cabinet.

American law student Chester Carlson invents xerography, the first method of copying to be based on the properties of selenium; the first efforts are crude; many years of development lie ahead before he has a commercial product.

Alan Turing writes "On Computable Numbers" describing a Turing machine that can solve all problems that are computable; John Atanasoff starts work on the first electronic computer, but the first prototype is not completed until 1939; and an operational version known as the ABC, which failed frequently because of problems with the punched card input, is not working until 1942.

Mathematician Georges Stibitz, working for the Bell Telephone Laboratories, developes the first binary circuit, a combination of batteries, lights, and wires based on Boolean algebra that can add two binary numbers; calls the device the "model K" or "kitchen adder" because he built it in his kitchen; this circuit becomes instrumental in the development of subsequent electromechanical computers at Bell Labs.

Brothers Russel H. and Sigurd Fergus Varian develop the klystron, a vacuum tube capable of generating microwaves and which will be used in radar transmitters.

The British Government begins construction of a chain of twenty radar "watching" stations along the east coast of Great Britain.

Frank Whittle and A.A. Griffith build the first working jet engine in England; the same year in

Germany, von Ohain and M. Muller independently develop a similar engine.

At a Peenemiinde, Germany, research station, Werner von Braun is one of the leaders of a team performing the first rocket tests.

Grote Reber builds in his back yard the first intentional radio-telescope, a 31-foot diameter dish, with which he begins to receive signals from space.

Technology was not the only "happening" arena in 1937, not by any means. In the US, the Wall Street stock market declined, signaling serious economic recession. In Chicago, there were four killed and 84 injured in the strike against Republic Steel. In Lakehurst, New Jersey, 36 of the 97 people on board died when the zeppelin *Hindenberg* burned in a hydrogen fire while trying to land. The disaster was captured on film and was reported in the first transcontinental radio broadcast. The same year, the first worldwide program heard in the US was the coronation of George VI, King of Great Britain.

The political backdrop crackled with change.

The Royal Commission on Palestine recommended the establishment of Arab and Jewish states. Italy withdrew from the League of Nations. Spanish rebels took Malaga, destroyed Guernica, and Gijón. Japan seized Peking, Tientsin, Shanghai, Nanking, and Hangchow; Chiang Kai-shek united with Communists, led by Mao Tse-tung and Chou En-lai. President Franklin D. Roosevelt signed US Neutrality Act.

There were wins and losses everywhere.

The Duke of Windsor married Wallis Simpson; George Gershwin died; Amelia Earhart was lost on a Pacific flight; Vanessa Redgrave was born. Joe Louis regained the world heavyweight boxing title, defeating James J. Braddock; the US Tennis team won the Davis Cup from England; and New York (AL) won the World Series, 4–1, defeating New York (NL).

In Harlem, the deeply religious Powells brought their son, Colin Luther, to St. Phillip's Episcopal Church to be baptized, the same church where their daughter, Marilyn, had been baptized in 1931.

6

I had a great childhood.

—COLIN POWELL

He was a tagalong brother, really a pretty average boy.

—MARILYN POWELL BERNS

In 1942, the Powells moved from Harlem to the South Bronx, to Fox Street, and then, in 1943, to Kelly Street. Education was the key, and Kelly Street meant access to good schools. Arie had graduated from high school; Luther had not. And when Arie differed with him on some matter, or wished to carry a point, she would remind her husband that she was the one with the diploma.

In terms of New York attitudes about neighborhoods, the move was also a move up socially, from segregated Harlem to an integrated neighborhood in the Hunts Point section of the South Bronx, where the Powells would continue to work for financial security and a better life.

The neighborhood offered block after block of comfortable brownstone apartments and orderly rows of single-family houses, and for the financially better-off, there were larger, more elaborate homes.

Although the police precinct where the Powells lived is the same one shown in the 1981 movie *Fort Apache, The Bronx,* starring Paul Newman, the extreme social breakdown depicted in the film was yet to come. Yes, there were burglaries; the residents certainly locked their doors. Yes, drug use was on the rise. Street fights and knifings occurred, and gangs armed with bottles, bricks, and zip guns waged turf wars. Yet, Powell recalls that "a certain rough-edged racial tolerance prevailed. And critically, most families were intact and secure."

He himself found the South Bronx an exciting place to be growing up particularly in a family that had "so many other cousins around that it really was sort of a floating family of lots of cousins who were almost like siblings to us all, and all of the parents of this extended family were pretty much the same."

At 952 Kelly Street, the Powells occupied the third floor of the four-story brick building which had eight apartments in all, two families to a floor. The block of Kelly Street next to the Powells' was slightly curved, and the neighborhood had been known for years as "Banana Kelly."

The ethnic makeup of Banana Kelly was heavily Jewish, mixed with Irish, Polish, Italian, black, and Hispanic families. The requisite corner candy store also had school supplies, ice cream, soft drinks, and the daily papers—here the *Daily News*, the *Post*, and the *Mirror*; the *New York Times* was not in demand in Banana Kelly. There were Jewish bakeries, Puerto Rican grocery stores, and Italian shoe repair shops.

Anyone who has lived in New York knows that as big as the city is, as overwhelming as it may seem from the outside, it is really a collection of neighborhoods, small, distinct communities, where people of varied backgrounds and temperaments live in social harmony, where a stranger is a stranger and a resident is a "belonger." Sometimes the neighborhood ends at the corner, or across the street; other times, the border is two doors before the corner but three blocks up. The neighborhood is very much like the classic village or small town: everyone knows everything about everyone; and in the face of a threat or danger, everyone looks out for you.

Powell's boyhood home was absolute center. "When I stepped out the door onto Kelly Street, I saw my whole world. You went left three blocks to my grade school, one more block to my junior high school." Between the two stood St. Margaret's Episcopal Church, where Luther Powell was senior warden, Arie headed the altar guild, Marilyn played the piano at children's services, Colin served as an altar boy, and the family had their own pew.

"I was a contented kid," Powell recalls, "growing up in the warmth and security of the concentric circles my family formed. At the center stood my parents. In the next circle were my mother's sisters and their families. My father's only sibling in America, Aunt Beryl, formed the next circle by herself. These circles rippled out in diminishing degrees of kinship, but maintained considerable closeness. Family members looked out for, prodded, and propped up each other."

7

Home is where one starts from.

—T. S. ELIOT
Four Quartets, East Coker

When the family moved to the South Bronx, and a year later, to Banana Kelly, the world that young Powell couldn't see from his front door was growing wilder and, in many cases, getting closer.

It is 1942.

The Japanese capture Singapore, Java, and Rangoon; occupy Bataan. More that 100,000 Japanese-Americans are transferred by the US government from the West Coast to inland camps; Major General Jimmy Doolittle bombs Tokyo; the Americans win the Battle of the Coral Sea and Midway; MacArthur is appointed Commander-in-Chief, Far East; 400,000 American troops land in French North Africa; and the FBI captures eight German saboteurs who land in Florida and New York.

Albert Speer is named German armament minister; the murder of millions of Jews in the Nazi gas chambers begins; the Germans reach Stalingrad.

Enrico Fermi splits the atom; magnetic recording tape is invented; Bell Aircraft tests the first US jet plane.

From T.S. Eliot, *Four Quartets*; from Thornton Wilder, *The Skin of Our Teeth*, wins Pulitzer Prize for drama; from Erich Fromm, *The Fear of Freedom*. George M. Cohan, John Barrymore, and Carole Lombard die.

Sugar rationing begins in the US; rents are frozen; gasoline and coffee are rationed as well.

Popular songs include *Praise the Lord and Pass the Ammunition*, *That Old Black Magic*, and *White Christmas*.

Joe Louis knocks out Buddy Baer and retains the world heavyweight boxing crown.

The following year, the Powell family moves to Kelly Street.

It is 1943.

Hitler orders "scorched earth" policy. Allied armies in North Africa are placed under Eisenhower's command. Allies land in Salerno Bay and invade Italy; Italy declares war on Germany; Russians take Kiev; US forces regain islands in the Pacific; Allied "round-the-clock" bombing of Germany begins.

President Roosevelt freezes wages, salaries, and prices to forestall inflation; shoe rationing begins in the US, followed by rationing of meat, cheese, fats, and all canned foods.

Race riots break out in several major US cities whose labor populations are bolstered by the influx of Southern blacks; the US War Labor Board orders coal mines to be taken over by the government when half a million miners strike.

Penicillin is successfully used in the treatment of chronic diseases; streptomycin is discovered; Nikola Tesla dies, as does George Washington Carver, the "Wizard of Tuskegee," black agronomist and founder of the Tuskegee Institute.

Jackson Pollock gives his first one-man show; Charlie Chaplin marries Oona O'Neill; *Casablanca* wins the Academy Award; Rodgers and

Hammerstein's *Oklahoma!* opens on Broadway. The zoot suit becomes popular attire among US hepcats, and the lindyhop yields to the jitterbug.

On Kelly Street, Colin Powell attends grade school at P.S. 39 and plays street games with his friends. In addition to the several dozen street games like stickball, punchball, and sluggo, they invent "kite fighting," their own version of World War II dogfights, and often scan the rooftops for the Messerschmitts or Heinkels that might materialize suddenly in the skies above them, on a mission to bomb Banana Kelly.

8

Collie, get yourself an education someday. Don't count too much on the store.

—JAY SICKSER

It's always darkest just before they turn on the lights.

—MOONFACE MARTIN
in Cole Porter's *Anything Goes*

In 1946, when Colin Powell was nine and still a student at P.S. 39, "I passed from the third to the fourth grade, but into the bottom form, called 'Four Up,' a euphemism meaning the kid is a little slow."

For the Powells, this was tantamount to disaster. From day one they had emphasized education as the key to surmounting the limitations that would otherwise deny their children the opportunities for advancement, the good life that was America's promise. Marilyn was already an excellent student, headed for college, but Colin was encountering difficulties as early as the fourth grade. Marilyn, it seems, was the curious one, the one who asked all the questions, What does that sign say? How do you spell—? But her brother, she said, "could have cared less." She has described him as an average or not quite average student in school, while Powell himself recalls, "I lacked drive, not ability. I was a happy-go-lucky kid, amenable, amiable, and aimless."

While the Powell family dealt with nine-year-old Colin's passing "Four Up," the world beyond Banana Kelly dealt with the comparative quiet of the aftermath of war. This in what was a brief spot in time between the end of what has been called the electric age and the onset of the electronic age the following year.

It is 1946. There are transitions, resolutions, restorations.

A 21-nation Peace Conference is held in Paris.

Truce is declared in the Chinese Civil War; Albania, Hungary, Transjordan, and Bulgaria become independent states; Britain and France evacuate Lebanon.

Charles DeGaulle resigns from the French presidency and is succeeded by Bidault; Klement Gottwald becomes Premier of Czechoslovakia; Dimitrov becomes premier of Bulgaria.

East German Social Democrats merge with Communists.

Power in Japan is transferred from the Emperor to an elected assembly.

Victor Emmanuel III abdicates as King of Italy and is succeeded by his son, Umberto II; an Italian referendum is in favor of a republic; Umberto II leaves the country; de Gasperi becomes head of state.

Juan Péron is elected President of Argentina.

The UN General Assembly holds its first session in London; Norway's Trygve Lie is elected Secretary-General; New York is declared the permanent UN headquarters; John D. Rockefeller, Jr., donates $8.5 million to the UN for the site of a permanent headquarters in New York City.

President Truman creates the Atomic Energy Commission. The UN Atomic Energy Commission approves US plan for control.

Churchill gives his "Iron Curtain" speech in Fulton, Missouri.

Verdict of the Nuremburg Tribunal: Ribbentrop, Goering, and ten other Nazis are sentenced to death; Hess and Funk, life imprisonment; Schacht and von Papen, acquitted; Goering commits suicide on the evening before his execution.

Films that year include William Wyler's *The Best Years of Our Lives*, Cocteau's *La Belle et la Bête*, Hitchcock's *Notorious*, Charles Vidor's *Gilda*, and David Lean's *Great Expectations*.

Robert Penn Warren is awarded the Pulitzer Prize for his novel, *All the King's Men*; from Arthur Miller comes *All My Sons*; from Lillian Hellman, *Another Part of the Forest;* from Eugene O'Neill, *The Iceman Cometh*; from John Hersey, *Hiroshima*; from Benjamin Spock, M.D., *Baby and Child Care*.

Benjamin Britten's opera, *The Rape of Lucretia*, is produced at Glyndebourne; from Gian Carlo Menotti, *The Medium;* the Salzburg Festival reopens.

On Broadway, Irving Berlin's musical comedy *Annie Get Your Gun* and Alan Jay Lerner and Frederick Loewe's *Brigadoon* open.

Pope Pius XII creates 32 new cardinals; Francis Xavier Cabrini (1850–1917) is canonized.

Gerhart Hauptmann, Damon Runyon, Booth Tarkington, Gertrude Stein, John Maynard

Keynes, US boxer Jack Johnson, Alfred Stieglitz, and W.C. Fields die.

The British Arts Council is inaugurated; London Airport opens, as does the New Bodleian Library, Oxford.

Couture wins against Walton with one punch in 10.5 seconds, the shortest recorded boxing fight in history; and Joe Louis successfully defends his world heavyweight boxing title for the 23rd time.

Technology continues apace.

The US Navy first tests an atomic bomb at Bikini. The test site lends its name to a bathing suit, a brief halter and separate bottom, which appears in France on July 5, spreads gradually to beaches around the world, and reaches the US in the 1960s.

The first mobile telephones are introduced; as is the first zoom lens, by Zoomar; the Gaggia company in Italy introduces an espresso machine that uses steam under pressure to produce strong coffee of low caffeine content; the Fender Guitar Company introduces the modern electric guitar with a solid body and various built-in controls.

The innovative Tucker Torpedo automobile,

with its engine in the rear and a third front headlight, is introduced by Preston Tucker, but by the following year, the company has produced only 51 cars, and collapses.

Appleton discovers that sun spots emit radio waves; a pilotless rocket missile is constructed by Fairey Aviation Company; the first Soviet nuclear reactor goes into operation on Christmas eve.

Maurice Wilkes developes an early version of Assembler, a mnemotechnic language that simplifies the programming of computers.

ENIAC, the first all-purpose, all-electronic computer is demonstrated to scientists and industrialists. Developed secretly during World War II, ENIAC does not use binary numerals, but has its vacuum tubes arranged to display decimal numerals; it draws so much electricity that it causes the lights in a nearby town to dim each time it is used. Early press releases claimed such feats as multiplying 360 ten-digit numbers or extracting a square root "in a single second."

The population of the US is 140 million.

Four years later, in 1950, it is 150,697,999.

By 1950, Colin had completed grade school, attended Intermediate School 52, and, while still directionless, was at least changing direction. To get to Morris High School, he had to walk out of his house and turn right for a few blocks instead of left.

In the wake of Marilyn's having attended Walton High School, the Powells urged their son to try for the equally prestigious Stuyvesant High. To this day, Powell has the report card showing the guidance counselor's advice against such an attempt. "Morris High, on the other hand," recalls Powell, "was like Robert Frost's definition of home, the place where, when you show up, they have to let you in."

He maintained a C average in high school despite his continuing to not have the slightest idea what he wanted to do with his life. He might be uncertain which profession to aim for, but he was determined not to fail his subjects, which would mean failing his parents. Their expectation that he would do better than they had, go further than they had, was a constant in his youth, and their understanding that education meant opportunity was part and parcel of their expectation. "Strive for a good education," they told him. "Make something of your life."

And if he admittedly "horsed around" in high

school and sometimes lagged in his studies, he was hardly idle.

On the recreational front, Powell hung out with "the guys," their customary route being from Kelly Street, up 163rd Street around Southern Boulevard to Westchester Avenue, and back home. Saturday mornings would find them at the Tiffany Theatre for a serial and a cowboy movie double bill. On Sundays he attended St. Margaret's Church with his family and still remembers the ceremonies, the pageantry, and the stirring drama of the traditional liturgy. The holiday incense might threaten to asphyxiate his sister, but Colin was a fervent acolyte, an enchanted participant—he loved the imagery and the poetry of it.

After school, Powell worked. He tells of a day when he was fourteen, on an errand for his mother which took him past Sickser's, a baby furnishings and toy store. The store owner, Jay Sickser, asked whether he wanted to earn a few bucks. There was a full truck backed up to the warehouse behind the store, and Powell was to unload the merchandise for the Christmas season. When Sickser came back a while later to see how Powell was doing, he found that the job was nearly finished. "So you're a worker," he said to Powell, in his thick Yiddish accent. "You want to come back tomorrow?"

Powell did, and his association with Sickser's continued for several years, during which Powell began to pick up Yiddish from the store's many Jewish customers.

In February of 1954, "thanks to an accelerated school program rather than any brilliance on my part," Powell graduated from Morris High School. He was two months shy of his seventeenth birthday, a good kid with an easy smile and a good worker with a knack for unloading prams at Sickser's. But so far he had not excelled at anything, nor had anything managed to ignite him, let alone consume him.

9

That's where the money is.

—ARIE POWELL

An honor student at Walton High, Powell's sister, Marilyn, had gone on to Buffalo State Teacher's College in western New York. Her departure from Grand Central Station on the Empire State Express had been the Powell family equivalent of the launching of the *Queen Mary*. True to form, Marilyn had excelled as an undergraduate as well. Hers was unarguably a hard act to follow. Still, despite a less than sterling high school average of 78.3, young Powell began looking at colleges. His sister's example and his parents' unswerving expectation with regard to education as a critical factor left him little room to do otherwise.

There was more than one reason for Arie and Luther to be so determined in the cause of education. At the time they arrived in New York and set up a household in Harlem, few people of color lived anywhere but Harlem. Among them were nearly 50,000 West Indians, who might vary in accents, religion, and customs from one another, depending on the island of origin—Jamaica or Barbados, for example—but who, in the aggregate, as a component of the black population, were characterized by a sense of pride, ambition, and a determination to achieve financial security and independence. As one biographer of Powell's, Carl Senna, observes, "In Harlem it was often said that when a Jamaican got 'ten cents above a beggar' he invested it in a business, in his family, or in a profession. And in Harlem one-third of the doctors, dentists, and lawyers were of West Indian ancestry."

Powell himself observes that "American blacks sometimes regard Americans of West Indian origin as uppity and arrogant. The feeling, I imagine, grows out of an impressive record of accomplishment by West Indians." By way of tracing that success, Powell cites the British ending slavery in the Caribbean in 1833, a generation before America followed suit. Also, the British stewardship had been by colonial rather than by home rule, meaning that they had been largely absentee landlords, leaving the West Indians pretty much on their own. "Their lives were hard but they did not experience the crippling paternalism of the American plantation system, with white masters controlling every waking moment of a slave's life. After the British ended slavery, they told my ancestors that they were now British citizens with all the rights of any subject of the crown. That was an exaggeration: still, the British did establish good schools and made attendance mandatory."

For Arie and Luther Powell, who had worked hard all their lives, education for their children would spell the difference between the routines they had known as shipping clerk and garment trade pieceworker and a genuine profession. What's more, there was plenty of evidence in the family for education being the foundation for a life of accomplishment.

Colin Powell's family, his blood relatives, and his extended family of lesser kin, number among them Arthur Lewis, a cousin, who followed a career as a Navy enlisted man with an appointment as US ambassador to Sierra Leone; Arthur's brother, Roger, was a successful architect; another cousin, Victor Roque, was a prominent attorney. Powell's cousin James Watson became a judge on the US Customs Court of International Trade; Watson's sister Barbara became the US ambassador to Malaysia and the first woman assistant secretary of state, and his sister Grace, an official in the Department of Education. Another of Powell's cousins, Dorothy Cropper, became a New York State Court of Claims judge, and his cousin Claret Forbes, one of the last to emigrate from Jamaica, is a nurse with two children in Ivy League colleges. Marilyn's daughter, Leslie, an artist, earned her Master's degree from Yale. And yet another cousin, Bruce Llewellyn, is a businessman, philanthropist, former senior political appointee in the Carter administration, and one of this country's wealthiest African-Americans.

Although it begins to look like becoming a professional was a prerequisite to full cousinhood, Powell's family also included subway motormen for the New York Transit System, while others were of an entrepreneurial persuasion and owned small businesses, and still others had clerical jobs. Whatever line of work they chose, work they did, and work hard, becoming good providers and parents whose way of life was characterized by purpose—to improve their station, to keep their families together, to educate their children to continue to grow and prosper.

As Powell sees it, in *My American Journey*, "I look at my aunts and uncles, their children and their children's children, and I see three generations of constructive, productive, self-reliant members of society. And all my relatives, whatever their professional status, enjoy equal standing in the family. No cousin stands above another in respect or affection. Some have experienced disappointment. Some did not achieve the success they desired. But they have all been successful in what counts in the end: they are useful human beings, useful to themselves, to their families, and to their communities."

There seemed to be two possibilities at the time, and Powell applied to both of them, New York University and the City College of New York, which was known at the time as CCNY, but would later become part of the City University of New York (CUNY). In what came as a surprise to Powell, given his lacklustre academic performance in high school, he was accepted at both colleges. His choice between the two boiled down to the dollars involved. NYU was a private school and in 1954, a year's tuition was a hefty $750. CCNY was a public school, with a nominal tuition of $10 for New York students. That was clear enough. He chose CCNY.

The next matter, what to study when he got there, was not so cut and dried. Powell was still without an inkling.

Arie put on her vocational counselor cap. After consulting the family—two more Powell cousins, this time Vernon and Roy, were then studying engineering—Arie advised Powell to go where the money was. Despite what he describes as an allergy to science and math, Powell agreed to enter as an engineering major.

10

Time present and time past
Are both perhaps present in time future,
And time future contained in time past.

—T. S. ELIOT
Four Quartets, Burnt Norton

—Anybody know what time it is?
—You mean now?

—YOGI BERRA

For someone without a clear—or even an unclear—notion of where he was headed, of what might speak clearly to him, draw him in, engineering was as good a choice of major as any other at the time, and in some ways, better than most. These were the boom years of the fifties. The demand for consumer goods was accelerating, and that meant an equally strong demand for the engineers to design the refrigerators, automobiles, and hi-fi sets that were creating such excitement among the country's consumers.

It is 1954. There are alliances and realliances.

British, French, US, and USSR foreign ministers meet in Berlin; the Russians reject the idea of German reunification. Eisenhower and Churchill meet in Washington and sign the Potomac Charter.

Dien Bien Phu taken by Vietnamese Communists; Indo-China armistice signed at Geneva; the French give up their rule and the Communists take over in Hanoi.

The Southeast Asia Treaty Organization (SEATO) is established.

Colonel Nasser seizes power in Egypt, becomes premier and head of state; Malenkov becomes Premier of USSR; Theodor Heuss elected President of West Germany.

US signs defense agreement with Japan; Burma and Japan sign treaty; US signs pact with Nationalist China; France and West Germany sign cultural and economic agreement.

Queen Elizabeth II and Prince Philip begin a tour of the Commonwealth; Marshall Tito visits

Greece and India; Emperor Haile Selassie of Ethiopia is in Bonn.

US and Canada agree to build radar warning stations across northern Canada (Distant Early Warning, "DEW" Line) to give warning of approaching aircraft or missiles over the Arctic.

President Eisenhower approves the St. Lawrence Seaway project.

Senator Joseph R. McCarthy continues his witch-hunting activities culminating in a nationally televised hearing seeking to prove Communist infiltration into the US Army; his formal censure and condemnation by Senate resolution follow.

US Supreme Court rules that segregation by color in public schools is a violation of the 14th Amendment to the Constitution.

The energy front remains active, even volatile as the US explodes the first true hydrogen bomb on Bikini Atoll in the South Pacific and US atomic physicist J. Robert Oppenheimer is labeled a security risk, dismissed from government service, and denied access to nuclear information.

The first atomic-powered submarine, the USS

Nautilus, built by Admiral Hyman G. Rickover, is commissioned.

The Soviet Union completes the first small nuclear reactor that is intended primarily to produce electric power; the United Kingdom Atomic Energy Authority is founded, its aim being the development of civilian applications of nuclear power; the US Atomic Energy Act allows private companies to build nuclear reactors and to maintain stocks of nuclear fuels.

There is concern in Europe and America about fallout and the disposal of radioactive waste.

Bell Telephone scientists develop the silicon photovoltaic cell, which can produce electric power from sunlight; the Association for Applied Solar Energy is founded in the US and publishes the periodical *The Sun at Work.*

There is plenty of movement in other areas as well. The first vertical-takeoff plane is developed in Great Britain; it is known as the "Flying Bedstead."

When Malcolm McLean begins transporting goods between New York City and Houston in containers that can be loaded onto trucks and ships, container transport spreads rapidly throughout the world and will displace most other forms of goods transport.

The pressure cooker, originally invented in the 17th century by Denis Papin, is reinvented by Frédéric, Jean, and Henri Lescure. In the US, TV dinners are introduced.

Automation has arrived.

Ford builds a 40-worker plant for engine blocks that has the same output as an older factory which needed 117 workers; Raytheon's new radio plant replaces 200 workers with two, who, between them, assemble 1,000 radios a day; and a machine for forming cups from aluminum strips replaces 55 workers with one.

The electronic age is here too.

Gordon Teal at Texas Instruments introduces the silicon transistor, which is much cheaper to manufacture than previously used germanium-based versions; and the first transistor radio, the Regency, appears on the market with a $49.95 price tag. It is not only smaller than any tube radio, it is cheaper.

And the computer age is not far off.

John Backus publishes a preliminary report, *Specifications for the IBM mathematical FORmula*

TRANslating system—FORTRAN, which marks the beginning of the development of true programming languages. Earl Masterson develops the Uniprinter for use with computers; called a line printer, it can execute 600 lines per minute.

The US has six percent of the world's population but 60 percent of all cars, 58 percent of all telephones, 45 percent of all radio sets, and 34 percent of all railroads.

The Independent Television Authority is established in Britain; Eurovision network is formed.

Twenty-nine million US homes have TV.

The Nobel Prize for Medicine and Physiology is awarded to J. F. Enders, T. H. Weiler, and F. Robbins for their work on the polio virus; Dr. Jonas Salk, developer of antipolio vaccine, starts inoculating school children in Pittsburgh, Pennsylvania. The Nobel Prize for Chemistry goes to Linus Pauling for his study of molecular forces. Chlorpromazine (Thorazine) is introduced for the treatment of mental disorders.

The Nobel Prize for Literature is awarded to Ernest Hemingway. Pulitzer prizes are awarded to: [Poetry] Theodore Roethke for *The Waking:*

Poems 1933-1953; [Biography] Charles A. Lindbergh for *The Spirit of St. Louis;* [History] Bruce Catton for *A Stillness at Appomattox;* [Opera] Gian Carlo Menotti for *The Saint of Bleecker Street;* [Drama] Tennessee Williams for *Cat on a Hot Tin Roof;* [Cartoons] Herblock, for the second time; [Music] Quincy Porter for *Concerto for Two Pianos and Orchestra.*

William Walton's opera *Troilus and Cressida* opens in London; Benjamen Britten's *The Turn of the Screw,* in Vienna; Schönberg's *Moses and Aaron,* in Hamburg; and Aaron Copland's *The Tender Land,* in New York.

The First (annual) Jazz Festival is held at Newport, Rhode Island. *The Boyfriend* and *Pajama Game* open on Broadway; *On the Waterfront* wins the Academy Award; popular songs are *Hernando's Hideaway, Mister Sandman, Young at Heart,* and *Three Coins in a Fountain.*

Dylan Thomas's *Under Milk Wood* is published posthumously. From Françoise Sagan, *Bonjour Tristesse;* from Kingsley Amis, *Lucky Jim;* from Mac Hyman, *No Time for Sergeants;* from John Patrick, *Teahouse of the August Moon;* from Enid Bagnold, *The Chalk Garden;* from Giraudoux,

Ondine; from Terence Rattigan, *Separate Tables;* from Thornton Wilder, *The Matchmaker;* from Aldous Huxley, *The Doors of Perception.*

William Golding writes *Lord of the Flies;* J. R. R. Tolkien writes *Lord of the Rings.*

In the visual arts, there is Chagall's *The Red Roofs,* Dubuffet's *Les Vagabonds,* Max Ernst's *Lonely,* Picasso's *Sylvette,* Lynn Chadwick's *Two Dancing Figures,* and Fernand Léger's *Acrobat and Horse.*

Arturo Toscanini retires; Viennese operetta composer Oskar Straus dies, as do conductors Wilhelm Furtwängler and Clemens Krauss, French novelist Colette, British philanthropist Seebohm Rowntree, Charles Ives, Lionel Barrymore, Reginald Marsh, and Henri Matisse.

Billy Graham holds evangelistic meetings in New York, London, and Berlin; Pope Pius X is proclaimed a saint by Pope Pius XII; and the World Council of Churches is convened at Evanston, Illinois.

In Morocco, a desert locust plague destroys citrus crops valued at $14 million in six weeks. In the City of London, the Temple of Mithras is excavated.

Roger Bannister runs a mile in 3 minutes 59.4

seconds; Arnold Palmer wins the US Golf Association's Amateur championship; the Philadelphia Athletics baseball club moves to Kansas City; and New York (NL) wins the World Series 4-0 over Cleveland (AL).

The cold war notwithstanding, the world is fired up. Things are popping. If many inventions are the direct result of technological developments during World War II, the war has also speeded up the creation of new materials, such as artificial rubber, plastics, and synthetics. New pathways are opening up, new connections, new possibilities.

Colin Powell, uncertain of his future, nevertheless goes forth in search of it, perhaps not as warmly as the world might wish, but this is February of 1954, and this is the Bronx. Old man winter is still calling the shots.

11

The first stage of the mythological journey—which we have designated the call to adventure—signifies that destiny has summoned the hero and transferred his spiritual centre of gravity from within the pale of his society to a zone unknown. For those who have not refused the call, the first encounter of the hero-journey is with a protective figure, often a little old crone or old man, who provides the adventurer with amulets against the dragon forces he is about to pass. What such a figure represents is the benign, protecting power of destiny. Not infrequently, the supernatural helper is masculine in form, some wizard, hermit, shepherd, or smith, who appears, to supply amulets and advice that the hero will require.

—JOSEPH CAMPBELL
The Hero with a Thousand Faces

Hey, kid, you new?

—RAYMOND THE BAGEL MAN

If it hadn't been a cold, raw February day, Colin Powell would probably still have shivered, stopping at the corner of Convent and 141st Street, about to enter the City College of New York. Established in the previous century "to provide higher education for the children of the working class," CCNY was alma mater to New York's poorest and her most gifted, among them Dr. Jonas Salk; Supreme Court Justice Felix Frankfurter; muckraker novelist Upton Sinclair; actor Edward G. Robinson; playwright Paddy Chayefsky; *New York Times* editor Abe Rosenthal; novelist Bernard Malamud; labor leader A. Philip Randolph; Congress of Racial Equality national chairman, Roy Innis; New York City mayors Robert Wagner, Jr., Abraham Beame, and Edward Koch; and eight Nobel Prize winners.

Colin Powell was a seventeen-year-old, C-average student out of an undistinguished South Bronx high school who was there because he would not disappoint his family, not because CCNY was the gateway to some future he envisioned and was determined to prepare for. The harsh winds whipped around him; the Gothic structures rose before him; Powell was young, and cold, and daunted.

At this point, a friendly voice called out to him: *Hey, kid, you new?*

As Powell recalls him, Raymond the Bagel Man—unaccountably so called, since Raymond in fact sold pretzels—was a short, red-faced, weather-beaten man with gnarled hands, standing behind a steaming cart of the giant, soft, salty pretzels that tell the people on the street what the skyline tells the people on the plane, This is it, this is New York.

Powell bought a pretzel from Raymond, the two of them chatted briefly, and, somehow, the chill moved off. February remained cold, but CCNY was no longer so intimidating a prospect. For the next four-and-a-half years, Powell was a regular of Raymond's and to this day, "while my memory of most of my professors has faded, the memory of Raymond the Bagel Man remains undimmed."

As Powell entered the campus on his way to the main building, Sheppard Hall, he would have passed by an unremarkable old building, although, unlike his clear recall of Raymond the Bagel Man, he doesn't remember paying any attention to it at the time. This was the ROTC drill hall, and it would become the focus of his life for the next four years.

12

And what you thought you came for
Is only a shell, a husk of meaning.

Either you had no purpose,
Or the purpose is beyond the end you figured
And is altered in fulfillment.

—T. S. ELIOT
Four Quartets, Little Gidding

The venture may begin as a mere blunder, or still again, one may be only casually strolling, when some passing phenomenon catches the wandering eye and lures one away from the frequented paths of men.

—JOSEPH CAMPBELL
The Hero with a Thousand Faces

Powell's first semester as an engineering major was relatively painless, possibly because he would not be required to take any engineering courses until the following year. That summer, by way of preparing for the inevitable, he signed up for a course in mechanical drawing.

Imagine a classroom filled with students; it is summer school; it is New York; it is hot and humid. Imagine the instructor. He asks you to draw "a cone intersecting a plane in space." Try to concentrate. Ignore the sound of pencils moving across paper as everyone else in the classroom draws the requisite cone. Just concentrate. Ignore the sound of the instructor moving through the aisles, making his way toward you; ignore the sensation of his standing just behind you, looking over your shoulder; ignore his studying the blank page on your desk, waiting for your hand, pencil at the ready, to commit the cone to paper. Keep concentrating. It will come to you.

But it didn't. "For the life of me, I could not visualize a cone intersecting a plane in space. If this was engineering, the game was over."

Although he hadn't discussed it with them, or been made by them to feel uncomfortable about it, Powell was already certain that Luther and Arie were concerned about his lack of staying power, his inability to throw himself into something and ride it out. That being the case, he was prepared for their disappointment when he announced that the engineering major was a wash; he was switching to geology.

Geology? A black kid from the South Bronx wants to major in geology? Clearly he had rocks in his head.

But geology was less about studying the earth and more about staying in school. It may have seemed on the seriously irrelevant side to his family, but it had two things going for it; first, it wasn't engineering—a rock was a rock and never a cone; second, it would permit him to remain enrolled long enough to graduate, which meant fulfilling his parents' expectations, which meant the game was worth the candle.

During that first semester, before the summer session and the mechanical drawing fiasco, Powell had noticed something not so much peculiar as unexpected about the makeup of the student body. CCNY, a "hotbed of liberalism, radicalism, even some leftover communism from the thirties," was hardly the place you'd expect to meet much of a military presence. And yet, there they were, young guys on campus in uniform. It was just something that happened to catch his eye; he'd inquire about it that fall when he returned to school in his new manifestation as a geology major.

In the fall of 1954, Powell did more than just inquire about the Reserve Officers Training Corps (ROTC), he enrolled. He still isn't sure why. It could have been any number of things. Perhaps it was growing up during World War II and the Korean conflict; certainly the big screen images—*Back to Bataan, Thirty Seconds over Tokyo, Guadalcanal Diary, Pork Chop Hill, The Bridges at Toko-Ri*—had surrounded him during those formative years. And it was certainly true that the word was out, just ask anyone: If you're going to go, it's better to go as an officer.

Powell was issued his olive-drabs, donned them, and liked what he saw. As he remembers it in *My American Journey*, "At this point, not a single Kelly Street friend of mine was going to college. I was seventeen. I felt cut off and lonely. The uniform gave me a sense of belonging, and something I had never experienced all the while I was growing up; I felt distinctive."

Of the three campus military societies, he chose to pledge the Pershing Rifles. ROTC, and specifically his acceptance into the Pershing Rifles, turned on the lights for Powell. Nothing in his experience thus far had given him the sense of brotherhood, of camaraderie, of belonging that he found in the Pershing Rifles, and having found it, he knew that he had craved it all along.

At the end of the pledge period Powell was entitled to wear the distinctive blue-and-white shoulder cords and enamel crests on his uniform. With the realization that he was attracted by such forms and symbols came yet another understanding. In all of the aimlessness, the confusion that had preceded his joining ROTC, there *had* been something he had excelled at previously, something he also loved—his ecclesiastical duties as an acolyte and subdeacon at St. Margaret's. "The organization, tradition, hierarchy, pageantry, and purpose—a world, now that I think about it, not at all that unlike the Army."

In his junior year Powell enrolled in advanced ROTC. Ronald Brooks, a young black man and the son of a Harlem Baptist preacher, was an early model and a mentor for Powell. In his first two years, Ronnie had become a cadet sergeant; Powell became a cadet sergeant. In advanced

ROTC, Ronnie became a battalion commander; Powell became a battalion commander; Ronnie was a drillmaster; Powell became a drillmaster.

That summer, in 1957, Powell did a six-week stint at Fort Bragg, North Carolina, in a ROTC summer training session. His reputation as a crack drillmaster preceded him and upon arrival he was named acting company commander. Upon completion of the course he was honored as "Best Cadet, Company D." He still has the engraved desk set and recalls his elation, "I was bringing my parents something they had never had from me—proof, with my desk set, that I had at last excelled. And I had found something that I did well. I could lead."

Powell was twenty years old.

In the fall of 1957, he returned to CCNY, where his otherwise mediocre grades were shored up by his straight A's in ROTC, and learned he was to succeed Ronnie Brooks. He was going to be cadet colonel of the entire, thousand-strong CCNY regiment; on top of that, he was elected company commander of the Pershing Rifles.

On the evening of June 9, 1958, in CCNY's Aronowitz Auditorium, with the First Army band playing, Powell and his fellow classmates stepped on stage.

As Powell himself recalls it—

I, Colin Luther Powell, do solemnly swear that I will support and defend the Constitution of the United States against all enemies foreign and domestic and that I will well and faithfully discharge the duties of the office upon which I am about to enter, so help me God.

"We live in a more cynical age today. We are embarrassed by expressions of patriotism. But when I said those words almost four decades ago, they sent a shiver down my spine. They still do."

13

Once having traversed the threshold, the hero must survive a succession of trials. This is a favourite phase of the myth-adventure.

—JOSEPH CAMPBELL
The Hero with a Thousand Faces

As a "Distinguished Military Graduate," Powell was offered, and enthusiastically accepted, a regular rather than a reserve commission; he would serve three rather than two years of active duty. In June 1958, Colin Luther Powell, 2nd Lieutenant, US Army, reported to Fort Benning, Georgia, for eight weeks of basic infantry training followed by two months at Ranger school.

Powell has often told young officers that most of what he knows about military life he learned in those first eight weeks—

- The Army's first general order, *Take charge of this post and all government property in view.*
- The mission is primary, followed by taking care of your soldiers.
- Don't stand there. Do something!
- Lead by example.
- "No excuse, sir."
- Officers always eat last.
- Never forget, you are an American infantryman, the best.
- And never be without a watch, a pencil, and a notepad.

It was at Fort Benning that Powell first read an old poem by Colonel C. T. Lanham in which the poet describes the plight of the lowly foot soldier, going all the way back to the Roman legions, and describes the fear, the death that must be faced with blind obedience, ending—

I see these things,
Yet am I slave,
When banners flaunt and bugles blow,
Content to fill a soldier's grave,
For reasons I will never know.

Despite the sentimental appeal of the poem, it ran counter to one of the principles Powell was taught and wholeheartedly embraced at Fort Benning, that American soldiers must know the reason for their sacrifices. As Powell puts it, "Our GIs are not vassals or mercenaries. They are the nation's sons and daughters. We put their lives at risk only for worthy objectives. If the duty of the soldier is to risk his life, the responsibility of his leaders is not to spend that life in vain. In the post-Vietnam era, when I rose to a position where I had to recommend where to risk American lives, I never forgot that principle."

Powell completed basic training in the top ten of his class, went on to Ranger school in the north Georgia mountains, and then to airborne training. If he never has to parachute again, Powell says that will be fine with him, but he would never shy away from what must be done. "These experiences are rites of passage. Physical danger that people face and master together bonds them in some mystical way. And conquering one's deepest fears is exhilarating."

Having earned his paratrooper wings on top

of his black-and-gold Ranger tabs, he went home on leave "like someone returning from another planet, from the Deep South to Queens."

He was twenty-one years old. He had a girlfriend. His parents were proud of him. And he was about to see the world.

Powell had orders to report to the 3d Armored Division in Gelnhausen, West Germany, about twenty-five miles east of Frankfurt and forty-three miles west of the Soviet zone. He was assigned as a platoon leader to Company B, 2d Armored Rifle Battalion, 48th Infantry. It was his first field command, forty men.

He returned home on leave during the summer of 1959, then returned to Germany where he was promoted to first lieutenant and reassigned as executive officer, Delta Company, 2d Battalion, 48th Infantry.

If ROTC and Fort Benning had been about officers, Gelnhausen, for Powell, was "my indoctrination into what the Army is really about—soldiers. I came to understand GIs during my tour at Gelnhausen. I learned what made them tick."

In November 1960, while Powell was in Gelnhausen, there was a presidential election, the first in which Powell was old enough to vote. He hadn't seen the Nixon-Kennedy debates—not much of the campaign made it to Gelnhausen—but he did cast an absentee ballot for JFK. His decision wasn't the result of any in-depth analysis. It was simply that, "In those days, he and his party seemed to hold out a little more hope for a young man of my roots."

By the end of 1960, Powell had completed his two-year tour of duty and was the only lieutenant in the battalion commanding a company, a job usually reserved for a captain. He was asked to extend, but he was homesick, he had a girl he hadn't seen in sixteen months, and he was ready for a change.

He had entered the 48th Infantry a rookie, and was leaving as a fairly seasoned pro. He headed back home to New York City, just a few hours' drive from his next assignment: Fort Devens, Massachusetts, about thirty miles west of Boston.

14

> The Army was living the democratic ideal ahead of the rest of America. Beginning in the fifties, less discrimination, a truer merit system, and leveler playing fields existed inside the gates of our military posts than in any Southern city hall or Northern corporation. The Army, therefore, made it easier for me to love my country, with all its flaws, and to serve her with all my heart.
>
> —COLIN POWELL
> *My American Journey*

In January 1961 Powell reported to his second duty station, Fort Devens, Massachusetts. He was assigned to the Ist Battle Group, 4th Infantry, 2d Infantry Brigade, under the command of Brigadier General Joseph Stilwell, Jr.

Initially a liaison officer in the battle group headquarters, Powell was essentially a "gofer" for Major Richard D. Ellison, the group's S-3 officer, in charge of operations and training. From Ellison, Powell learned the fine art of proposal sorting—expediting the good, short-circuiting the bad, and squelching the ugly—while making sure their superiors remained copacetic. While Powell and Ellison became good friends, Powell eventually extricated himself from the liaison slot and became executive officer of Company A, which made him second in command. When the company commander was reassigned, Powell moved up. He was still a first lieutenant, but he was now in command of his second company since joining the Army. It was a short enough tour. Powell was soon made adjutant with a new unit, the Ist Battalion, 2d Infantry, and again he was a first lieutenant in a captain's job.

There were skills to be acquired, lessons to be learned, experience to be gained, but all things considered, Fort Devens was a possible two and Gelnhausen a ten on the excitement barometer. The Cold War ramparts in West Germany had it all over the cold weather in Massachusetts.

By the summer of 1961, Powell's obligatory three years of service were over and he could have left the Army. Instead, the adventure-starved young officer put together the necessary scratch for a round-trip air fare to the Caribbean and spent his leave in Jamaica, surrounded by a sea of aunts, uncles, and cousins he had never met but felt, now, as if he had lived among them from birth.

From the island of Jamaica he paid a visit to the borough of Queens, to 183–68 Elmira Avenue, a three-bedroom bungalow in Hollis, the home the Powells had always hoped, and in the late fifties had finally managed, to buy. At the time he had graduated from CCNY, Powell's parents had pretty much assumed that their son would complete his three years with Uncle Sam and then return to New York where he could begin making something of himself. The three years were over and Powell had come home. But he had only come home for a visit.

Leave the Army?

It was the farthest thing from his mind.

As Powell saw it, "I was in a profession that would allow me to go as far as my talents would take me. And for a black, no other avenue in American society offered so much opportunity. But nothing counted so much as the fact that I loved what I was doing. And so, much to my family's bewilderment, I told them I was not coming home."

Two days later, he was back at Fort Devens.

And if Army life wasn't quite as exciting as Powell might have liked, the world outside was whirling.

It is 1961.

John F. Kennedy is inaugurated as the 35th—and youngest ever—President of the US; he establishes the Peace Corps, meets with Harold Macmillan at Key West, Florida, and again in Bermuda, and visits Paris, Vienna, and London.

Queen Elizabeth II tours India, Pakistan, Persia, Cyprus, and Ghana.

Konrad Adenauer visits London.

US breaks off diplomatic relations with Cuba.

David Ben-Gurion forms a new coalition government in Israel; Edward Heath begins negotiations for British entry into the Common Market; the Berlin Wall is constructed, and vice-president Johnson visits Berlin.

Cuban-exiled rebels, trained and supplied by the US, attempt an unsuccessful invasion of Cuba at the Bay of Pigs; President Kennedy acknowledges his full responsibility for the fiasco.

Kennedy and Krushchev meet in Vienna to discuss disarmament, Laos, and Germany.

Elizabeth Gurley Flynn succeeds Eugene Dennis as Chairman of the US Communist Party; the activities of the reactionary John Birch Society are a concern of the US Senate; and the UN General Assembly condemns apartheid.

"Freedom Riders," white and black liberals loosely organized to test and force integration in the South are attacked and beaten by white citizens, men and women, in Anniston and Birmingham.

Yuri Gagarin orbits the earth in a six-ton satellite, and Alan Shepard makes the first US space flight.

JFK cancels the Air Force nuclear bomber project because he thinks cheaper and less problematic long-range missiles can accomplish the same goals.

Physicists Erwin Schrödinger and Percy Bridgman die, as do Ty Cobb, Gary Cooper, Dashiell Hammett, Ernest Hemingway, George S. Kaufman, James Thurber, Sir Thomas Beecham, Augustus John, Eero Saarinen, Grandma Moses (b. 1860), Carl Gustav Jung, and Dag Hammerskjöld, who is killed in a car accident.

Adolf Eichmann is found guilty in Jerusalem trial.

Rafael Trujillo, dictator of the Dominican Republic, is assassinated; he is succeeded by his son.

Sam Rayburn, elected Speaker of the House of Representatives for ten terms, dies; he is succeeded by John MacCormack.

Floyd Patterson retains the heavyweight boxing crown against challenger Ingemar Johansson; Bobby Fischer, 17, wins the US chess championship for the fourth time, defeating Paul Benko, Hungarian Grand Master.

In the US, FM radio stations begin broadcasting in stereophonic sound.

IBM completes the 7030 computer, with 169,100 transistors, for Los Alamos Laboratories, and introduces the Selectric typewriter, in which characters are printed on paper by a rotating ball while the carriage remains fixed.

Jack Lippes introduces an inert plastic intrauterine device (IUD) for birth control.

J. D. Salinger writes *Franny and Zooey;* by Jean Anouih, *Becket;* by Max Frisch, *Andorra;* by Mackinlay Kantor, *Spirit Lake;* by Joseph Heller, *Catch 22;* by Shelagh Delaney, *A Taste of Honey;* by Harold Robbins, *The Carpetbaggers;* by Robert

Heinlein, *Stranger in a Strange Land;* by John Steinbeck, *The Winter of Our Discontent;* by Iris Murdoch, *A Severed Head;* by Harold Pinter, *The Collection;* by John Whiting, *The Devils;* by Bernard Malamud, *A New Life;* by John Osborne, *Luther;* by James Baldwin, *The Me Nobody Knows.*

T. H. White is awarded the Pulitzer Prize for *The Making of the President: 1960,* and the Academy Award goes to *West Side Story.*

Michael Ramsey is appointed Archbishop of Canterbury; the New English Bible appears on the 350th anniversary of the Authorized Version; the World Council of Churches meets in Delhi; Moscow synagogues are closed.

Investigations in Scandinavia and the US Adirondack Mountains confirm that acidity is increasing in small lakes, killing some species; the cause is believed to be acid precipitation resulting from air pollution, which becomes known as "acid rain."

Nondairy coffee creamer is introduced.

Popular songs include *Moon River, Where the Boys Are, Exodus,* and *Love Makes the World Go Round.*

By late fall, love reached Colin Powell's part of the world.

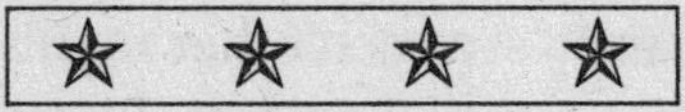

15

My name is Alma, Spanish for Soul.

—TENNESSEE WILLIAMS
Summer and Smoke

This blind date might just work out.

—COLIN POWELL
My American Journey

In November 1961 Colin Powell did a favor for Mike Heningburg. He'd never been on a blind date before, but Mike was a friend, Powell's dance card had been empty for a while, and, after all, it was just for the evening.

The two left Fort Devens for Boston, where Powell was introduced to Mike's girl, Jackie Fields, and Jackie's roommate, Alma Johnson. As Powell remembers it, Alma talked; he listened. She spoke graciously, with a soft Southern accent; he was entranced.

They began to see each other regularly and by the time Alma went home to Birmingham for the Christmas holidays, they agreed that she would return to Boston via New York so that she could meet Powell's family. In the new year, Alma began visiting Powell weekends at Fort Devens.

By the time Powell had been at Fort Devens for a year and a half, he was due for orders. It was August of 1962, and his orders came, right on schedule—Powell was headed for South Vietnam.

Not that he knew anything about the place. Only that President Kennedy had sent a few thousand men there as advisors, and that "we were involved in something called 'nation-building,' trying to help South Vietnam save itself from the Red Menace that stretched from the Berlin Wall to the rice paddies of Southeast Asia."

He would have a five-week military advisor course at Fort Bragg, North Carolina, that fall and could expect to be a captain by the time he shipped out.

Powell was beside himself; he was going to war.

He told his parents, he told his friends, and he told Alma. His excitement evidently didn't make it all the way across the telephone lines from Fort Devens to Boston; at least, there was no audible evidence of his enthusiasm having struck a chord. It was such good news! He went to see her, to make it clear to her. This was what he had been preparing for, and what's more, there was icing—a promotion to captain—on the cake.

He hadn't made Alma's day.

A pen pal for a year while he was in Vietnam was not something she saw for herself; if that was the deal, she was folding.

Powell was floored. Back at Fort Devens that night, he thought it through. The next day, he drove back to Boston and proposed to Alma.

"Thank God, she said yes."

They were married in Birmingham, Alabama, on August 25, 1962, in the Congregational Church, with a reception in the Johnson home. The Powells gave them a wedding reception not long afterward, at Elmira Avenue, and on September 24, a month after the wedding, the battalion gave them a farewell party.

They were off to Fort Bragg.

At Fort Bragg's Unconventional Warfare Center, prospective advisors were brought up to speed on Southeast Asia in a five-week intensive. The course covered colonial history, introductory language classes, and a review of events that had brought the Vietnamese situation to the present pass, or impasse.

In 1954, Powell had graduated from Morris High, met Raymond the Bagel Man, braved the imposing Gothic facades of CCNY, begun in engineering, encountered the recalcitrant cone, switched to geology, and landed in the open arms of ROTC and the Pershing Rifles.

In 1954, the French had given up their rule in what was then known as French Indochina, the Communists had taken over in Hanoi, and the Vietnamese people had resolved themselves into two countries, Communist North Vietnam and pro-Western South Vietnam. A long, drawn-out guerrilla war ensued, during which the Communist Viet Cong, encouraged and supported by North Vietnam, sought to overthrow the regime in South Vietnam and reunite the country under Communist rule.

In 1961, at year's end, there were three thousand-plus advisors in Vietnam.

In 1962, a US military council was established in South Vietnam, and at year's end, Powell and the group he was part of would swell the ranks of US special advisors to eleven thousand strong.

By December 1962, Powell had received his promotion to captain and he had completed the Military Assistance Training Advisor course. Powell and Alma, who was carrying their child, had decided that she would return to her family in Birmingham while Powell was away.

Four months after their marriage, and two days before Christmas, Powell left Birmingham for Travis Air Force Base in California. He arrived in Saigon on Christmas morning, 1962.

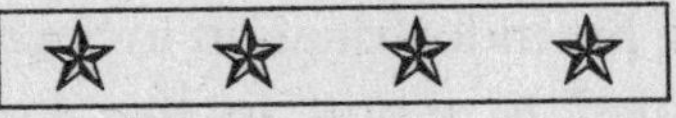

16

Not fare well,
But fare forward, voyagers.

—T. S. ELIOT
Four Quartets, Dry Salvages

Going forward seems like retreat.

—LAO TSU
Tao Te Ching

The day after Christmas, a disoriented group of special advisors, all newly arrived in Saigon, were given what Powell describes as "a rousing pep talk," reaffirming their mission to halt the Marxist advance, restoring their determination to help the South Vietnamese resist a communist takeover of their country. Their fervor thus rekindled, they were issued "field gear, jungle fatigues, jungle boots, helmets—reminders of where we were headed."

Following his indoctrination in Saigon, Powell was scheduled to report to the Army of the Republic of Vietnam (ARVN) and would serve as advisor to the four-hundred-man 2d Battalion, 3d Infantry Regiment, of the 1st Division, posted in the tropical forest along the Laotian border at A Shau.

When he finally reached A Shau—no small trick in the rainy season—Powell seems to have encountered yet another guardian at the threshold, a Southeast Asian variation on Raymond the Bagel Man.

Captain Vo Cong Hieu was a Vietnamese officer. As Powell recalls his ARVN counterpart, the man he would be advising, Hieu was "short, in his early thirties, with a broad face and an engaging smile. But for the uniform I would have taken him for a genial schoolteacher, not a professional soldier."

Captain Hieu accompanied Powell on a preliminary tour of the compound. When Powell gestured to the mountain that towered over the A Shau post, Hieu identified it as "Laos."

The ensuing exchange, reported in full by Powell in his book, *My American Journey*, became for Powell an emblem of the circular reasoning, the Alice-in-Wonderland logic that riddled the Vietnam experience.

In brief, Powell wondered why the post had been established in such a vulnerable spot; Hieu assured him it was a very important outpost and it was here to protect the airfield. Powell asked what the airfield was here for; Hieu explained that the airfield was here to resupply the outpost.

In all of the wrestling Powell would do with the US experience in Vietnam, that may have been as much sense as Vietnam ever made: *We're here because we're here because we're here.*

Powell was there, that first time, for eleven months.

His son was born March 23, 1963, in the Holy Family Catholic Hospital in Birmingham. In April, Powell got word of the birth. In May, the pilot of an L-19 observation plane radioed Powell that a special-delivery package was on its way down to him. From the drop zone, Powell retrieved a box of candy, inside which was an envelope, inside which was a photograph of Michael Kevin Powell.

In July, Powell stepped into a punji trap and the spike pierced his boot and passed through his sole to the top of his instep. He was flown to Hue, treated, and though he recovered quickly enough, his days as a field advisor were over.

He was reassigned to Ist ARVN Division headquarters as assistant advisor on the operations staff. As an additional duty he was assigned as commander of the Hue Citadel airfield. In an incident involving a pilot who apparently resented a nonaviator running his airfield, Powell accepted a challenge to go for a spin and then had to order the pilot to return to the field when his aerial capers brought the two over North Vietnam. Powell dates one of his cardinal rules from this experience: *Don't be buffaloed. Experts often possess more data than judgment.*

17

For God's sake, let us sit upon the ground
And tell sad stories of the death of kings—

—WILLIAM SHAKESPEARE
Richard II

The returning hero must survive the impact with the world.

—JOSEPH CAMPBELL
The Hero with a Thousand Faces

On November 1, 1963, Powell was in Saigon, his tour over, waiting to be processed out so he could head for home.

The city had been placed under martial law in August, and a week later, President Diem had extended that to the whole country. But today, it was clear to Powell that something more serious was in progress. Troops in personnel carriers were the only traffic in the streets; the

Presidential Palace had been damaged by arms fire.

Powell had arrived in Saigon in the middle of a coup.

The government had just been overthrown by a cabal of South Vietnamese generals. President Diem and his brother, Ngo Dinh Nhu, the secret police chief, had been assassinated.

Powell was twenty-six years old, politically unsophisticated, and regarded the coup as one more baffling event in a land where little that he had seen had made any sense.

Three weeks later, Powell had managed to leave Saigon and was on the last leg of a long journey home.

He was sitting in an airport in Nashville, Tennessee, waiting for his flight to Birmingham, when an unusual stillness overcame the customary hustle. The arrival and departure boards had been quietly abandoned; travelers were gathered around a television set in the airport lounge.

It was November 22, 1963, and that afternoon John F. Kennedy, the President of Powell's own country, had been murdered in Dallas.

Nothing made sense.

18

What life have you if you have not life together?

—T. S. ELIOT
Choruses from "The Rock"

Hi, Mike, I'm your Pop!

—COLIN POWELL
My American Journey

In Birmingham, Powell was met by Alma—"She looked beautiful and vaguely familiar"—and was introduced to his son.

The homecoming celebration with Alma's family was followed by a Christmas visit with the Powell family on Elmira Avenue in Queens, where Michael's battle with acute croup left Michael the victor and his father, a shaken survivor.

The next stop was Fort Benning, Georgia,

where Powell began a Pathfinder course, advanced airborne Ranger training, to fill part of the eight months that remained until August 1964, when his assignment to the Infantry Officers Advanced Course was slated to begin. Once the "career course" started, Powell would be entitled to government housing. In the meantime, he went looking—this was Georgia, he was limited to black neighborhoods—and with the help of a black real estate agent, finally found a house with a yard for the baby in Phenix City, across the border in Alabama.

As Powell remembers it in *My American Journey*, he had been going back and forth between the house, which he was fixing up for Alma and Mike, and the Fort Benning BOQ, where he was bunking. One night, on the way back to the post, he pulled into a drive-in hamburger stand on Victory Drive. He knew they wouldn't serve him inside, so he waited in his car until a waitress came out to the car window. He asked for a hamburger.

Was he Puerto Rican?

No.

Was he an African student?

No.

Powell thought she seemed to be genuinely trying to help.

"I'm a Negro. I'm an American. And I'm an Army officer," Powell told her.

She replied that she herself was from New Jersey, didn't really understand any of this, but she was not allowed to serve him. If he would go behind the restaurant, she would pass him a hamburger out the back window.

"I'm not *that* hungry," he told her, burning rubber as he backed out.

"My emotional reaction, or at least revealing my emotions this way, was not my style. Ordinarily, I was not looking for trouble. I was not marching, demonstrating, or taking part in sit-ins. My eye was on an Army career for myself and a good life for my family. For me, the real world began on the post. I regarded military installations in the South as healthy cells in an otherwise sick body. If I hurried, I could get to the snack bar or the officers' club before closing and be served, just like everybody else."

The Pathfinders are paratroopers who jump in ahead of airborne and heliborne assault units to mark landing and drop zones. The Pathfinder course was incredibly demanding and it came as a surprise as well as a great honor when Powell learned that he was graduating number one in his class.

In the six months that still remained until the Infantry Officers Advanced Course began, the Army came up with yet another interim assignment, "test officer" with the Infantry Board at Fort Benning. The job was testing new weapons and equipment for acceptability by infantry standards: did it work? how available was it? what were the cost and effort required to keep it working?

At the conclusion of his junket, Powell was asked whether he would like to return to the Infantry Board when he had completed the career course, which, for Powell, would mean being able to stay on at Fort Benning. An Infantry Board testing officer didn't have quite the ring to it that the Rangers, Green Berets, and airborne elites had, but Powell was adapting happily to a stable home life, and he said Yes, he'd be pleased to return.

While Powell had been testing weapons and equipment for the Army at Fort Benning, President Lyndon Baines Johnson had signed the Civil Rights Act, outlawing discrimination in places of public accommodation.

That summer, in August 1964, Powell began the Infantry Officers Advanced Course, the so-called career course, which was designed to prepare infantry captains to take over command of a company and serve on a battalion staff. Between Germany, Fort Devens, and Vietnam, Powell had already had the required experience, but the course itself was required and what's more, it meant he could now bring his family into government housing on the post.

That same summer, Powell returned to the hamburger joint and ordered a hamburger without being told to go around to the back.

In the fall of 1964, LBJ ran for president against conservative Republican candidate Barry Goldwater, who had cast the lone vote in the Senate against the civil rights bill—on constitutional grounds, not out of racism. All the same, his opposition was fuel for the segregationists' fires.

Powell slapped a red-white-and-blue "All the Way with LBJ" bumper sticker on his Volkswagen.

"Shortly before election day, November 3, 1964, I mailed in my absentee ballot to my New York voting address. LBJ, all the way. And I treated myself to another burger on Victory Drive."

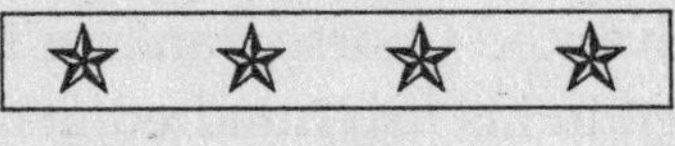

19

> I came to understand that a movement requires many different voices, and the tirades of the agitators were like a fire bell ringing in the night, waking up defenders of the status quo with the message that change had better be on the way.
>
> —COLIN POWELL
> *My American Journey*

Fort Benning is the home of the infantry, and Powell was an infantryman. Life settled down for a while, and Powell describes the time as one of the happiest in his life.

On April 16, 1965, at Martin Army Hospital, their second child, Linda Powell, arrived. This time, Powell was there from the get-go, determined to catch up on everything he had missed on his first round as a parent.

In May 1965, Powell finished the Infantry

Officers Advanced Course, ranking first among infantry men in his two-hundred-man class and third in the combined group of four hundred participants. He returned to the Infantry Board after the course, as per plan, and spent several months evaluating new infantry equipment.

In the spring of 1966, he was ordered to report to Infantry Hall, where he had recently been a student. When Powell left Southeast Asia in 1963, it had been a Vietnamese conflict involving some 16,000 American advisors. Now the American involvement had swollen to 300,000 troops, and the Army needed more officers. Powell had been assigned to the faculty.

He completed an instructors' course, again first in his class, and entered his own classroom, wearing an oak leaf. It had taken Powell only eight years to attain a rank usually reached after ten or eleven years. What's more, Army officers are divided into three broad categories: company grade, field grade, and general officers. Powell had just made field grade. He was in a whole new league.

Powell had been teaching for nearly a year when he learned that, instead of a second posting to Vietnam—which, with the war dragging on, was bound to happen sooner or later—he would be going to the Army Command and General Staff College at Fort Leavenworth, Kansas, a career turning point. If the career course had been the Army equivalent of a bachelor's degree, Leavenworth was a master's. By the time the thirty-eight week course had ended, he and his classmates would be expected to know how to move a division of twelve to fifteen thousand men by train or road, how to feed it, supply it, and above all, fight with it.

During his time at Leavenworth, a relative stability and steady progress marked his own life and that of his family. It was at Leavenworth that Alma, baptized a Congregationalist, became an Episcopalian, because she and Powell were committed to growing together spiritually as a family.

Still, the time was punctuated by milestones of continuing political and social unrest.

On February 1, 1968, Powell was stunned, as was all of Leavenworth, to see telecasts of American GIs fighting on the grounds of the US embassy and ARVN forces battling before the Presidential Palace in the heart of Saigon. The Viet Cong, with the support of the North Vietnamese Army, had struck 108 of South Vietnam's provincial and district capitals. The campaign was launched on the eve of the Vietnamese lunar New Year, Tet—hence its name in history as the Tet offensive.

On March 31, 1968, President Johnson told the country that he would not seek reelection. The country was dangerously divided and Johnson could not hold it together.

Five days later, in April 1968, the Reverend Martin Luther King, Jr., was murdered in Memphis.

Not long afterward, Powell's orders came through, and on July 21, 1968, he was once more on his way to Vietnam.

20

No one starts a war, or rather no one in his senses should do so, without first being clear in his mind what he intends to achieve by that war and how he intends to achieve it.

—KARL VON CLAUSEWITZ
On War

War should be the politics of last resort.

—COLIN POWELL
My American Journey

On July 27, 1968, Powell arrived at Duc Pho, assigned to the 23rd Infantry Division, known as the Americal. He was to serve as executive officer of the 3d Battalion, Ist Infantry, IIth Infantry Brigade.

His duties, which he describes as bean counting for the annual inspection, shifted when Major General Charles M. Gettys, up in Chu

Lai, commanding the Americal Division, saw Powell's photograph in a two-month-old issue of the *Army Times*. Gettys reportedly told his staff, "I've got the number two Leavenworth graduate in my division and he's stuck out in the boonies as a battalion exec? Bring him up here. I want him for my plans exec."

As chance would have it, however, General Gettys had another vacancy, the G-3 spot, one of the most coveted jobs, and one which usually goes to the "fastest burner" among the lieutenant colonels in a division. Gettys had to fill the spot immediately and he decided to take a chance on Powell.

"The general's decision enormously influenced my career," says Powell. "Overnight, I went from looking after eight hundred men to planning warfare for nearly eighteen thousand troops, artillery units, aviation battalions, and a fleet of 450 helicopters."

In November 1968, a helicopter carrying Powell and several others, among them General Gettys, crashed while trying to land in a small jungle clearing. The gunner and Powell, who was sitting outboard, jumped clear of the wreck but went back when they saw that no one else was moving. Powell climbed in, and managed to drag Gettys into the woods. Several soldiers on the ground joined them, going back for the rest of the victims and pulling them to safety before the helicopter exploded and burned.

Back at Chu Lai base hospital, x-rays revealed that Powell's ankle was broken. The Army doesn't evacuate G-3 officers for broken bones, so Powell donned a cast and prepared to spend his second Christmas in Vietnam.

By the time Powell's second tour ended, in July 1969, he had held down the G-3 spot for the largest division in Vietnam, a rare credit for a major. He had received the Legion of Merit, and the Soldier's Medal for his role in the helicopter crash rescue.

But that was Vietnam as experienced by what Powell calls "the career lobe" of his brain. "As time passed and my perspective enlarged, another part of my brain began examining the experience more penetratingly."

In his book, *My American Journey*, Powell takes the time to share some of his reflections on Vietnam at length. Among his many observations is one that dates from his first tour and the outpost at A Shau.

"In the years between my first and second tours, the logic of Captain Hieu's explanation—the base is here to protect the airstrip, which is here to supply the base—had not changed, only widened. We're here because we're here because. . . ."

On June 15, 1969, Powell learned he had been accepted for the fall class in the School of Government and Business Administration at The George Washington University.

On July 20, 1969, Powell was back in the States, in Atlanta, where he and Alma were spending a few days before joining the kids and Alma's folks in Birmingham.

That evening, Powell was absolutely clear on two things: more than anything else, he wanted to get home and see his children; and, there was no way he could keep his eyes open another minute, not even for the astronauts who were walking on the moon.

21

I began to experience the Imposter Syndrome. What am I doing here?

—COLIN POWELL
My American Journey

Out of the military, back to civilian life, and for the first time, a home of their own. In the fall of 1969, the Powells went about reentry.

The Army agreed to two years and two summer sessions instead of the original eighteen months for the course of study, and Powell plunged into the rigors of academic life in the MBA program at The George Washington University (GWU) in Washington, D.C. Daunted he may have been, but he was determined as well, and his first-semester grades were straight A's—until the spectre of the Cone returned to haunt him.

In an exam for a computer logic course, he was asked to illustrate, by means of a flow chart of a software program, how the computer made decisions. Suddenly, he was back at CCNY, trying to visualize a cone intersecting a plane in space. Despite his D in the midterm, Powell managed to wind up with a B in the course, "probably through divine intervention."

On May 20, 1970, the Powells' third child, Annemarie was born.

In July 1970, Powell learned that he was to be promoted to lieutenant colonel the following month.

In September 1970, Powell was back at GWU, in chinos and a sports shirt, feeling like an undercover agent in the enemy camp. He was a professional soldier in college at the height of the antiwar movement.

On April 24, 1971, more than 200,000 antiwar demonstrators gathered on Capitol Hill to pressure Congress to get us out of Vietnam, and Powell watched as hundreds of Vietnam Veterans Against the War threw their ribbons and medals at the building.

Powell skipped the graduation ceremonies in

May and picked up his degree from the dean's office.

He had earned straight A's, a lone B in computer logic, and declined a suggestion that he stay on for a Ph.D.

It was time to get back to the Army.

22

There has never been a protracted war from which a country has benefited.

—SUN TZU
The Art of War

Because of the controversy over Vietnam, the American military had become alienated from its own people, which struck me as unhealthy in a democracy.

—COLIN POWELL
My American Journey

In July 1971, his MBA secured, Powell reported to the Pentagon, assigned to A-Vice, the office of the assistant vice chief of staff of the Army, who was at that time Lieutenant General William E. DePuy.

As President Nixon began the process of withdrawal from Vietnam, military thinking was widely influenced by a *sub rosa* document known as the Carlisle report, a survey by the Army War College in Carlisle, Pennsylvania, of 450 lieutenant colonels, nearly all of whom had served in Vietnam. The report, in a nut shell, cited the Army's significant failures and squarely blamed the Army itself—particularly the senior leadership—for a massive failure of integrity and wholesale subscription to a facade of illusion and delusion. "Change," insisted the report, "must be instituted from the top of the Army."

DePuy, who was known as one of the toughest generals to come out of Vietnam, "was not happy with our doctrine, structure, or leadership or the ethical climate of the Army in the wake of the Vietnam debacle." He was determined to rethink, and remake, the role and structure of the US Army, to which end he had gathered around him his own personal "brain trust" of the sharpest lieutenant colonels he could find.

Powell had visions of himself installing computer systems for A-Vice; after all, that was the main skill he had been sent to grad school to acquire. "Our lives, however, turn on chance," says Powell. Colonel Francis G. "Goose" Gosling took a look at Powell's record and said there was no reason for Powell to be drawing computer flow charts when he could be helping General DePuy design tomorrow's Army, thus sparing the Army an undistinguished computer hacker and exposing Powell, at a key point in his career, to the best and brightest, in one of the most prestigious and promising offices in the Pentagon.

In November 1971, while Powell was still in DePuy's office, he received a call from the Infantry Branch telling him to expect an eight-page application for a White House Fellowship which was to be completed by that weekend. It didn't matter to Infantry Branch that Powell wasn't interested; he was being drafted.

The White House Fellows program had been operative for seven years at that point, and had proven highly effective in its continuing objective—"to expose young comers, particularly from the private sector, to the federal government at the highest level. The goal was to give future American leaders a better appreciation of how public policy was shaped and how their government operated."

A few weeks later, Powell was notified that he

had made the first cut from the original 1,500 applicants. He was one of 130 who would be interviewed. Following the initial interviews, thirty-three finalists were chosen and, after a three-day final selection process at Airlie House, in Virginia, Powell was notified that he was one of the seventeen selected by the President's Commission to serve as a 1972-73 White House Fellow.

23

This'll blow over.

—FRED MALEK

The question of where to spend his year as a White House Fellow never really came up for Powell. It was the Office of Management and Budget (OMB) for him.

If his MBA courses and his time at the Pentagon had taught him anything at all, it was simply this—

"Budgets are to organizations what blood is to the circulatory system. And OMB had its hand on every department's jugular. It is one of the least understood yet most powerful federal agencies in Washington."

Powell was interviewed by Frank Carlucci, the deputy to the director, Caspar Weinberger, was accepted as the OMB White House Fellow, and introduced to another member of the Weinberger team, William Howard Taft IV, a grandson of the 27th President of the United States.

Although the trio left not long after Powell's arrival, Weinberger to become head of the Department of Health, Education, and Welfare (HEW); and Carlucci, his deputy; and Taft, his counsel—they were impressed with Powell's competence and his quiet efficiency and, down the line, would figure prominently in Powell's career.

The new deputy director of the OMB was Fred Malek, a West Point and Harvard Business School graduate with a reputation as a hatchet man. A phone call from Fred Malek was like a phone call from the Mafia; chances were good it was the last call you'd ever get.

As Malek's special assistant, Powell became the gatekeeper. To get to Malek, you had to go through Powell.

In the Fred Malek school of management Powell received a thorough grounding in the day-to-day operations of the federal bureaucracy, of which the OMB was the nerve center.

While the cabinet officials were out making the speeches, the OMB was running the show.

In January of 1973, the White House Fellows traveled to the Soviet Union and, the following June, to China.

As the White House Fellows' year drew to a close, Malek talked to Powell about staying on for another year at OMB. Powell knew that the education he had received in the past year was beyond any he could have hoped for in any school of political science or public administration in the country, but he had been away from soldiering for over three years and he preferred not to continue his "detour from a straight-line military career path."

In the background, recalls Powell, the television set in Malek's office was tuned to the Watergate investigating subcommittee, and Malek told him, "This'll blow over."

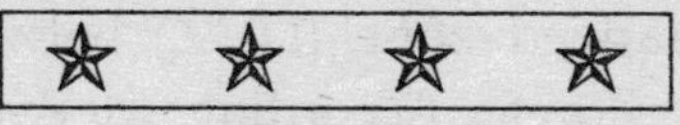

24

You hear what Bro P did? Whacked Biggs. Biggs is gone, man, gone. You don't mess with Bro P.

—The word around Camp Casey

In 1973, now a lieutenant colonel, Powell took command of the 1st Battalion, 32d Infantry, 2d Infantry Division, Eighth Army, Korea. He would be at Camp Casey for a year.

His new commanding officer, Major General Henry E. "The Gunfighter" Emerson, had taken over the 2d Division at Camp Casey just a few months previously, and he had found the morale low, the discipline slack; Gunfighter had come into a tough command.

The armistice in Korea had been agreed to on July 27, 1953. Twenty years later, the US was still there. Camp Casey was twenty-five miles from the demilitarized zone (DMZ) between North and South Korea. According to Powell, "The 2d Infantry Division was there, to put it bluntly, to provide a buffer of American flesh and blood."

Drugs and racial tension plagued the division. Apparently white officers and noncoms had no problem cracking down on white troublemakers, but they often backed off in the case of recalcitrant blacks lest they be labeled racists. Powell had no such qualms.

"Bro P" had become Powell's nickname, at least among the black troops, when he had defused a tense situation with a young soldier, who was either drunk or doped up. Powell had talked him down from homicidal maniac to confused kid, and the soldier, a few weeks later, had thrown him a salute, telling his friends, "That's Bro P, Brother Powell, he's all right."

One particularly telling incident recalled in *My American Journey* involved a black corporal whom Powell, for the sake of the story, calls "Biggs."

Powell was advised by his command sergeant major, Albert Pettigrew, that a new man, a Corporal Biggs, had just gotten himself transferred to Camp Casey, and he looked like trouble.

Got himself transferred?

Pettigrew explained that Biggs had managed to have orders cut sending him wherever he wanted to go.

Powell wanted to see this soldier.

Biggs, a small, cocky-looking guy, soon reported to Powell and told him he was really glad to be down here because, as he informed Powell in a confidential tone, there were serious racial problems here, but he thought he could handle them.

Powell explained how he ran his battalion, but the next thing Powell knew, Biggs was holding meetings of black troops behind the barracks, issuing dire warnings of what white officers would do if blacks did not stand up to them, and using drugs to manipulate himself into a position of control.

Powell asked for Biggs's file, studied it, and then called the corporal into his office again.

How're you doing, Biggs?

Sir, the battalion's got more trouble than I thought. I got here just in time. We ought to get together every day to talk things over.

That won't be possible, Corporal. There's a plane at Osan and you are going to be on it today. That plane is going to Travis Air Force Base in California, and when you get off, some people will be waiting with your discharge papers. And they're going to put you out the gate.

You can't do that to me! Biggs protested.

I've already done it. You are out of my battalion. Out of this brigade. Out of this division. Out of this man's Army. And you are unemployed.

Word went out to the battalion: "You hear what Bro P did? Whacked Biggs. That's right. Biggs is gone, man, gone. You don't mess with Bro P."

It had taken determination, decisiveness, energy, and imagination, but Powell had cleaned up the Korean battalion and was universally praised by blacks and whites for his fairness in doing it.

"I threw the bums out of the Army and put the drug users in jail," he said. "The rest, we ran four miles every morning, and by night they were too tired to get into trouble."

His success as a problem solver in his Korean command, focusing on the restoration of military morale, authority, and discipline, won him another appointment to the Pentagon in 1974.

25

> The rivalry among the services produces both the friction that lowers performance and the distinctiveness that lifts performance. The challenge, then, now, and forever, is to strike the right balance.
>
> —COLIN POWELL
> *My American Journey*

> Colin, you're not going to have a conventional Army career. Some officers are just not destined for it.
>
> —MAJOR GENERAL JOHN WICKHAM

Powell had been in Korea, crouching in the mud on a Gunfighter Emerson morale-boosting maneuver, when he got word that he had been chosen for the National War College (NWC), the Harvard of military education, at Fort McNair, Washington, DC.

In September 1974, a month after President

Nixon had resigned from office in the wake of the Watergate scandal, Powell returned from his tour in Korea.

In August 1975, NWC classes would start.

In the interim, Powell was assigned to the Pentagon, where William Brehm, assistant secretary of defense for manpower, reserve affairs, and logistics put him to work analyzing military manpower requirements for the department's annual projection. Working with career Pentagon civilians, under Irving Greenburg, Powell had his first shot at juggling the needs, and the rivalries, of the Army, the Air Force, the Navy, and the Marine Corps.

Powell recalls working like a dog, going through endless drafts, and celebrating the day when the report was submitted to Congress—ahead of schedule—and he was off to the National War College.

In February 1976, Powell received an accelerated promotion to full colonel. Soon afterward, there was more good news. After the war college, he would assume command of the 2d Brigade of the 101st Airborne Division at Fort Campbell,

Kentucky. He was the youngest in his war college class to make colonel and one of only two Army officers in the class chosen for brigade command.

A year later, in February of 1977, Powell was "happily immersed" in commanding troops when he was called to Washington to be interviewed for a National Security Council job by newly inaugurated President Jimmy Carter's National Security Advisor, Zbigniew Brzezinski.

"Here we go again, I thought, off the career track."

At Fort Campbell, Powell felt he was doing something he loved to do and needed to do, validate himself once again as a true infantry officer. The 101st Airborne, the "Screaming Eagles," was a storybook division and it had captured his heart; he hated the idea of leaving.

Powell consulted his superior officer, Major General John Wickham, who was skilled in the ways of the Washington labyrinth, and was told to go to Washington and at least talk to Brzezinski.

Powell met with Brzezinski, who wanted him

to run the NSC's defense program staff. Powell was flattered but not interested. Brzezinski became more enthusiastic; Powell continued to demur. Finally, Brzezinski told him they'd talk again when Powell was closer to the end of his command. It might not be the same job they were discussing now, but they wanted him.

Back at Fort Campbell, when Powell told General Wickham about the trip, Wickham said, "Colin, you didn't take this job, but they'll be back, or somebody else will."

As Powell's command of Fort Campbell wound to a close, Dr. Brzezinski again asked Powell to come to Washington. Since the job he had originally offered Powell had been filled, by Victor Utgoff, Brzezinski now wanted Powell to take the job as Utgoff's assistant.

Powell was hardly champing at the bit and said he'd need some time to think it over.

He then received another call, from the Pentagon this time, to see John Kester, Special Assistant to the Secretary and the Deputy Secretary of Defense. Kester had created a four-person team of military officers to help him gain control over a sprawling bureaucracy and ride herd on the Joint Chiefs of Staff, and he wanted Powell to run the unit as his executive assistant.

"I now had two high-level job offers," recalls Powell, "neither of which I wanted."

He consulted Wickham and another friend, Carl Vuono, a fellow DePuy protégé who had recently been promoted to brigadier general and was now working for the Army Chief of Staff, General Bernard Rogers. Vuono sounded out General Rogers and the answer came back—"We want Powell in Kester's operation." Powell expressed his regrets to Brzezinski and went to work for Kester.

26

Colin, don't be surprised if you end up as Chairman of the Joint Chiefs of Staff someday.

—W. GRAHAM CLAYTOR, JR.

The sage is guided by what he feels and not what he sees. He lets go of that and chooses this.

—LAO TSU
Tao Te Ching

In December of 1978, nearly a year and a half after he'd begun working for Kester in the Department of Defense, Kester and Charles Duncan, General Brown's deputy secretary, appeared at Powell's office door, both grinning widely.

Kester congratulated Powell and told him he'd been made brigadier general.

Duncan congratulated Powell and told him he

wanted Powell to come to work for him as his military assistant.

On June 1, 1979, there was a formal promotion ceremony in the elegant dining room of the Secretary of Defense. The room was filled with family and friends, some from previous posts, some even from ROTC. Charles Duncan did the honors.

"The one gaping hole was Pop."

Luther Theophilus Powell had died the previous spring, in April 1978, at home, on Elmira Avenue.

"Still I felt that he was up there somewhere strutting among the other souls saying, 'Of course, what did you expect?' "

The promotion made Powell, at age forty-two, the youngest general in the Army.

Charles Duncan and Powell had become good friends, and one evening Duncan confided to Powell that the Carter administration was in for some changes. President Carter was determined to renew the nation's battered spirits, which was going to mean some shake-ups in the cabinet. Among others, Joseph Califano, Secretary of

Health, Education, and Welfare, and James Schlesinger, Secretary of Energy, would be leaving. Carter had asked Duncan to take over the Department of Energy (DOE).

Powell would miss Duncan, but here it was, his chance to escape the front office and get back to the Army.

At that point, Duncan continued: "And I want you to come with me."

Before Powell could get any ways into an objection, Duncan stopped him. He had already cleared it with the new Army Chief of Staff, General Edward "Shy" Meyer, and he promised Powell he would cut him loose as soon as he had gotten his feet wet at DOE.

Duncan was as good as his word, but Powell wound up with one more stretch between him and the Army, this time for W. Graham Claytor, Jr., previously Secretary of the Navy, and now Duncan's replacement as the number two man at Defense. Claytor wanted Powell for his military assistant, working with Claytor's current assistant, Navy Captain Jack Baldwin. Army Chief of Staff General "Shy" Meyer saw Powell's being in place as a tactical advantage—there would be an Army man on board.

By now, Powell had toured the Middle East, and before he was released to the Army once more, he would have an insider's view of Desert One, a failed attempt to rescue the fifty-three American hostages seized by Iranian "students" and held captive in the American embassy in Teheran.

Given his experience with helicopter operations in Vietnam, Korea, and the 101st Airborne, Powell was "surprised at the way this operation had been conceived and conducted. I would have rated Desert One's chances of success at a hundred to one.

In 1987, Congress created the Special Operations Command (SOCOM) under a four-star general, to provide the planning, coordination, and supervision lacking in Desert One. In Just Cause, the mission to restore democracy to Panama, we were to find out how well this overhaul worked."

Powell stayed with Claytor another eight months, during which time Ronald Reagan was elected President.

In January of 1981, the ritual of administration

changeover saw Claytor and the rest of the Democratic Defense appointees cleaning out their desks. On his last day at the Pentagon, Claytor shook hands with Powell and said, "Colin, don't be surprised if you end up as Chairman of the Joint Chiefs of Staff someday."

Powell remembers thinking that as a compliment, it was nice; but as a prophecy, unlikely.

Among the replacement appointees were Caspar Weinberger as Secretary of Defense and, as Weinberger's number two, Frank Carlucci. Powell welcomed Carlucci to the department.

"Colin Powell," Carlucci said with a smile, "I remember you from the OMB. Good to see you again. You're going to be my military assistant, I understand."

A month later, the new Secretary of the Army, John O. Marsh, Jr., asked Powell to consider resigning from the military to become undersecretary of the Army. Marsh had checked it out with Carlucci and the White House personnel office and he had been given thumbs up.

Powell thanked him for the offer, declined, and began badgering Carlucci. He wanted out of

Washington and back to the Army. It took Powell a few more months, but he did it.

Carlucci threw a farewell party for Powell at which he awarded him the Defense Distinguished Service Medal, and the two parted close friends.

In 1981, Powell returned to the field, first as assistant division commander of the 4th Infantry Division (Mechanized) at Fort Carson, Colorado, and then, in 1982, as deputy commanding general, United States Army Combined Arms Combat Development Activity, Fort Leavenworth, Kansas.

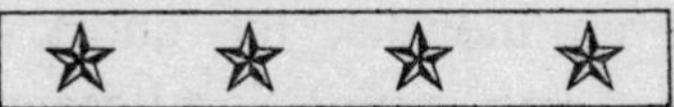

27

In a world bristling with engines of destruction, don't be surprised if they explode from time to time.

—COLIN POWELL
My American Journey

Generally, management of many is the same as management of few. It is a matter of organization.

—SUN TZU
The Art of War

By June 29, 1983, there was an up side and there was another side. Powell stood in Grant Auditorium while Lieutenant General Carl Vuono, now deputy commander of Training and Doctrine Command (TRADOC), pinned a second star on Powell. The promotion to major general was welcome, professionally and emotionally. That was the up side.

After eleven months, too short a stay, the Powell family was leaving Fort Leavenworth and returning, reluctantly, to Washington, D.C. That was the other side.

But from Washington's point of view, the bright, experienced officer had been away two years, and he was sorely missed in the defense establishment. It took several meetings, but Weinberger had finally managed to persuade Powell that he could best serve his country in Washington.

Powell became senior military adviser to Secretary of Defense Caspar Weinberger and worked for him for three years, during which time he acquired a reputation as a skilled assistant who could expedite the flow of information and get along with different groups of people. He also played an important role in several military operations, including the US invasion of Grenada in October 1983 and the 1986 raid on Libya.

One of the first incidents with which Powell had to deal was the downing by the Soviet Union of a Korean Air Lines flight #007, a commercial jet liner full of civilian passengers. When the Soviets tried to pass off KAL 007 as a spy plane, they added falsehood to what had been, at base, a tragic blunder.

Among the lessons Powell drew were: Don't be stampeded by first reports; don't let your judgments run ahead of your facts; and even with supposed facts, question them if they don't add up.

"I also learned that it is best to get the facts out as soon as possible, even when new facts contradict the old. Untidy truth is better than smooth lies that unravel in the end anyway. Be prepared to see an international event expand—or contract—for political ends apart from intrinsic meaning. And finally, in a world bristling with engines of destruction, don't be surprised if they explode from time to time."

Five years later, when Powell was National Security Advisor, the American cruiser USS *Vincennes* shot down an Iranian airbus, killing 290 passengers and crew. It was a tragic blunder, just as the downing of the KAL 007 had been. "We said so and released the facts publicly as fast as possible."

Powell's work at the Pentagon brought him power and influence in the US government. On March 25, 1986, he was awarded a third star, becoming, at the age of forty-nine, a lieutenant general, and he earned a job he had wanted for a long, long time. On July 2, 1986, Powell took over the US Army V Corps, headquartered in Frankfurt, West Germany. His first field command, twenty-five miles east of Frankfurt, at Gelnhausen, had been forty men. Now he was in charge of the 75,000-member V Corps, and he has said that while he was immersed in running the V Corps he was "probably the happiest general in the world."

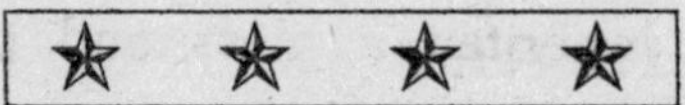

28

The hero may have to be brought back from his supernatural adventure by assistance from without. That is to say, the world may have to come and get him.

—JOSEPH CAMPBELL
The Hero with a Thousand Faces

Frank, you're gonna ruin my career.

—COLIN POWELL
To Frank Carlucci, in *My American Journey*

By the end of November 1986, in the wake of the Iran-contra affair, President Reagan had to appoint a new National Security Advisor, and his choice was Frank Carlucci. When Powell received a call from Carlucci, he congratulated him and would have preferred that the conversation end there. No such luck. Carlucci pressed Powell to come back to Washington as his deputy. He'd inherited a mess and he needed Powell's help with it.

Powell pleaded with him. It wasn't his mess; there must be a dozen guys he could ask; his foreign policy credentials were too thin.

Frank didn't want a foreign policy expert; he was looking for someone who could make things work, someone who could impose order on the NSC, someone who could do what Powell had already done for Carlucci and Weinberger. He wanted Powell.

Still Powell resisted, telling Carlucci that he was finally back in the real Army, and he wasn't ready to leave.

"I did not want to leave until I had proved I was an able corps commander. I did not want to be a guy who ran a company for a couple of months, a battalion and a brigade for a year, skipped a division, and ran out on a corps after just five months. And after the experience with Poindexter and North, I could not believe the country would stand for another military man in the NSC."

Carlucci said they'd talk again, and he rang off.

Then Weinberger called him. The pressure was on. Powell held out.

Two days later, Carlucci called back. He wanted Powell.

Powell told him it couldn't come from Carlucci. There was only one way that Powell could interrupt his command honorably, and that was in response to a direct request from his commander in chief. That would be the one thing Powell's world would understand.

Powell remembers the evening of December 12, 1986, quite clearly. He and Alma had just come home from a Christmas party and were sitting in the kitchen when the phone rang. The President was calling. "He said he knew how much the command meant to me, how happy Alma and I were in Frankfurt," but it was critical for the country that Powell come home. President Reagan needed him to help Carlucci straighten out the mess at the NSC.

And that settled that.

29

In speech, be true.
In ruling, be just.
In business, be competent.
In action, watch the timing.

—LAO TSU
Tao Te Ching

On December 18, 1986, Powell's appointment to the President for national security affairs was announced, and on the last day of that year, Powell formally gave up his command of V Corps.

Back in the US, the Powells were reunited with their children and the general's career continued to rise. From 1987 to 1989, the extent to which affairs ran smoothly and efficiently between the White House and the government agencies was due largely to Colin Powell.

Carlucci and Powell had similar approaches to security policy, and Carlucci often sent Powell to the White House to brief President Reagan. The personal relationship between Powell and Reagan grew, and in November 1987, when Carlucci succeeded Weinberger as Secretary of Defense, Reagan promoted Powell to National Security Advisor. He had become the first African-American to head the National Security Council.

Between the two of them, Carlucci and Powell pretty much saved the day for the Reagan administration, which was bogged down in the scandal surrounding the Iran-contra affair, while Russian leader Mikhail Gorbachev was impatiently seeking an end to the arms race.

While Carlucci ran interference with the cabinet officials and Congress, Powell took charge of the National Security Council, rebuilt the staff, and coordinated the work of the Pentagon, the State Department, and the CIA. There were frequent meetings with the press, in which Powell was adept, frank, and charming, and as he continued to work his magic in the National Security Council, Powell secured a firm position of trust within the Republican foreign policy establishment, despite the fact that no one seemed to know anything about Powell's party affiliation.

Just before the presidential election, Reagan signed the order promoting Powell to full four-star general, effective April 1989.

During the 1988 election campaign, Republican candidate George Bush turned to National Security Advisor Powell for something more than a briefing on arms-control negotiations. He wanted to appear familiar and at ease with the intricacies of US–Soviet negotiation; he wanted Powell to polish his image. At the final meeting between President Reagan and Premier Gorbachev on Governors Island, Powell set up the schedule so that Bush would have maximum photo presence standing with Reagan and Gorbachev. It was a masterful manipulation of public relations during the presidential campaign.

In January 1989, President-elect George Bush called Powell, thanked him for his services in the Reagan administration, and told him that he thought he ought to have his own National Security Advisor.

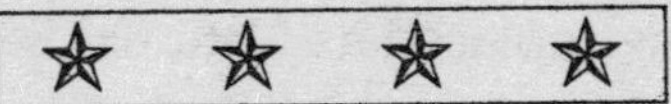

30

If nothing is impossible, then there are no limits. If a man knows no limits, then he is fit to be a ruler.

—LAO TSU
Tao Te Ching

I feel we are on the verge of something exciting. I somehow don't feel that we will settle into a comfortable rut living out our lives in Dale City with you coming and going to the Pentagon. . . . I don't know what is in store for us, but something big and exciting will happen.

—ALMA JOHNSON POWELL
Letter of August 13, 1974

Colin Powell likes lists.

Objectification is important to him, setting out the issues in a way that can be seen, studied, evaluated. Imagine a football coach setting out his strategy by making diagrams of players, positions, strategies. Imagine a general.

After being replaced as National Security Advisor following George Bush's election, two roads diverged for Powell. He could stay in the Army or he could leave. There were literally millions of reasons on each side.

A New York literary agent had told Powell that he could earn a million dollars a year on the lecture circuit, and that was the essence of the "Leave" list. This would be a compelling factor for many people, but for Powell it was just a single item with not much weight.

On the other side, the "Stay in the Army" list, was family. You can't belong to a lecture circuit. The Army had taken care of him and his for so long that leaving turned out to be unthinkable. It was a home he could not yet abandon. And, of course, he enjoyed the work.

So Powell stayed. In April 1989, General Carl Vuono, the Army Chief of Staff, offered him leadership of the US Forces Command at Fort McPherson in Atlanta. Powell had earned a fourth star and would now take command of all troops stationed in this country. His immediate extended family had just grown by nearly a million, including the active roster, the reserves, and the National Guard, and his annual budget was over ten billion dollars.

Although General Powell had achieved a significant measure of comfort and familiarity within the corridors of power in Washington, this was something new. He had just graduated from an important post in a tight network of influence and power into a position that commanded wholly different vistas. It's all a question of scale; visible, perceived scale. Here he was making decisions on a daily basis that would and did affect the living, working, training details of nearly a million lives, often in the most personal ways.

The job only lasted until August of that year, at which time George Bush offered Powell the chairmanship of the Joint Chiefs of Staff, but the importance of the position should not be overlooked. A man learns his worth in stages, by seeing himself grow, change venues, and rise to each occasion. A hero develops as much through the perception of others. When a man of honor has the ability to reach so many, to share with them, they all become shards of a single massive mirror to show him to himself.

Forces Command was a stage and a brief one, but also a staging arena for the next step up.

The Joint Chiefs of Staff is the agency responsible for advising the President on all military matters. In addition to the chairman, there is a vice chairman, the chief of naval operations, the commandant of the Marine Corps, and the chiefs of staff of the Air Force and the Army. These six people meet three times a week in a windowless room called "the tank." The chairman of this body holds the highest position of leadership in the nation's armed forces next only to the President himself. When confirmed by the Senate in October 1989, General Powell became the youngest man ever to hold that post, and the first African-American.

President Bush praised Powell as "a person of breadth, judgment, experience and total integrity," referring as well to Powell's military and scholarly distinction, appointing him, as it turned out, over the heads of several generals senior in rank to Powell, and for a double term of four years instead of the more usual two-year appointment.

In a speech to the fourteenth convention of the National Association of Black Journalists, Powell broadened his overt family yet again by acknowledging, in great detail, the contributions of those black officers who had preceded him, the "Buffalo Soldiers," Teddy Roosevelt's four black regiments in the Spanish-American War, as well as individual black officers, asserting that his appointment to the Joint Chiefs "would never have been possible without the sacrifice of those black soldiers who served this great nation in war for nearly three hundred years. Yes, I climbed and I climbed well and I climbed hard," said Powell. "I climbed over the backs and the contributions of those who went before me."

Targeting the young, Powell went on to position himself centrally among the generations gone and to come, "But now that I am on top of that cliff looking ahead, there are still some more hurdles to be crossed, and our young people have to be ready."

The images are both classic and classical, and eminently self-aware without being self-conscious.

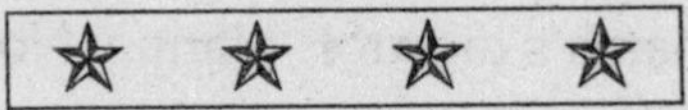

31

What we call the beginning is often the end
and to make an end is to make a beginning.
The end is where we start from.

—T. S. ELIOT
Four Quartets, Little Gidding

To rule truly is to serve.

—*The I Ching*

According to Powell, it was little more than twenty-four hours after he had become the Chairman of the Joint Chiefs of Staff when the first calls came in, alerting Powell to a coup brewing against the Noriega regime in Panama.

He told himself, Welcome back to the big leagues.

Powell monitored the situation closely, and when the time was right, on December 29, 1989, some 26,000 troops invaded Central America, ousting Panama's dictator, Manuel Noriega. The operation was an enormous success. Noriega was quickly captured and brought to Florida for trial. He was subsequently convicted and sentenced to prison. On January 4, Powell went to Panama to bring the US troops home. He wanted to be a hands-on leader.

In under 90 days, Powell had become a popular hero.

But Panama was just for starters.

More than anyone else, Powell is credited with the smooth planning, swift strike, superior firepower, and stunning success that characterized what has become known as Operation Desert Storm, or the Gulf War.

When Iraqi leader Saddam Hussein refused to withdraw from Kuwait by January 15, 1991, as ordered by the UN Security Council, Powell, in cooperation with General H. Norman Schwarzkopf, head of US forces in Saudi Arabia, launched Operation Desert Storm. Powell had started planning this the previous August, when troops from Iraq first invaded the neighboring country of Kuwait. Now his major task was to coordinate the combined efforts of the US and seventeen other nations who had committed the troops to the operation.

Following weeks of heavy bombing of military and government facilities in Iraq, a ground offensive began on February 24. Four days later Saddam Hussein, his army in full disarray, agreed to withdraw from Kuwait.

The Persian Gulf War ended in a cease-fire on February 28, 1991, having lasted forty-three days, with very few casualties to the US and its allies.

Both Powell and Schwarzkopf were hailed as national heroes, and Powell was even mentioned as a likely vice-presidential candidate in the 1992 election, but he declined to consider it, and chose instead to serve a new commander in chief, President Bill Clinton, in January 1993.

Powell's term as chairman of the Joint Chiefs of Staff ended eight months later. So did his life in the military. A soldier for thirty-five years, Powell announced his plans to retire from the Army on September 30, 1993.

For thirty-five years, Colin Luther Powell has served his country, has been a hero, time and time again. But now it's different. Because in the light of the fires over the Persian Gulf, at just that point in the arc of his life, when the man, and the time, and the eyes of all the world are perfectly aligned, at just that Promethean moment, he is lighted up for us, and we have now caught fire.

Retirement? Yes, from something he did or was or seemed before we saw him. Not retire from us. No, he is just beginning for us, and we for him. We're all in this together now.

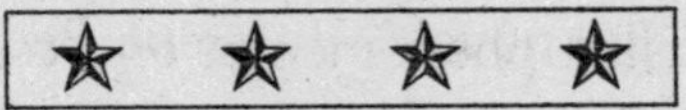

32

> We cannot revive old factions
> We cannot restore old policies
> Or follow an antique drum.
>
> —T. S. ELIOT
> *Four Quartets, Little Gidding*

> The community today is the planet, not the bounded nation. As the new symbols become visible, they will not be identical in the various parts of the globe; the circumstances of local life, race, and tradition must all be compounded in the effective forms. The way to become human is to learn to recognize the lineaments of God in all of the wonderful modulations of the face of man.
>
> —JOSEPH CAMPBELL
> *The Hero with a Thousand Faces*

We are at a special time in American history and in the history of mankind.

As the millenium approaches, we have an increasing awareness of our place in time. It is not an unusual phenomenon on occasions like this. We have something to mark, to celebrate. A milestone in our history.

There are other factors as well.

Technology has escalated so rapidly that we look to any reminder of stability, the timeless and timely myths by which our various cultures have lived, to remind us of who and what we basically are—human.

Our ability to destroy ourselves and each other has far outpaced the enlightenment of our governments and religions. Again, we need reminders, mirrors to tell us that we are good, that we are human.

We need desperately to believe in our own good, because, whether we like it or not, we do believe in evil. We have simply had too many examples in too short a time not to. Many try not to believe, but to no avail. It's in the movies we watch, the books we read, the news we see on television. Nostradamus, Patric Walker—they are with us everywhere we turn.

We suspect on some level, and fear very deeply, that a monumental battle between good and evil is coming. And, of course, we would all like to be on the right side.

How can we know? How can we be sure that God, glory, and the good are on our side?

Simple. That's what *heroes* are for. And that's why we need one—or more—now perhaps more than ever before.

There is every likelihood that Colin Luther Powell is not the answer, that he cannot fix the country, save America, level the playing field, make us all into the loving, caring, disciplined family we all recognize from the fifties sitcoms.

But we sure would like it if he could.

Colin Powell has participated, either as witness or as actor, in virtually every important event of this generation. His lifetime covers a span of years that bridges every generation gap. His military career reads almost like a history of modern warfare. In a time of increasing polarization, Powell stands for unity.

And best of all, Colin Powell is black.

After nearly a year and a half dominated by the racial and judicial ambiguities of the O.J.

Simpson media event, Colin Powell emerges from his self-imposed exile, his recluse state, his mythic cave, wielding a kind of bible for our times, his autobiography, the chronicle of his journey. He is the other side of O.J. He is our guardian. He is the liberal's dream, assuaging the white man's guilt with his very presence. In a brilliant reversal of archetypes, he is a black man in a white hat.

How could anyone be on the side of good and not like him?

Again, we are discussing perceptions, influences, a remarkable man's remarkable popularity. Only he can decide what to do with all this at this particular point in time.

But he must know that the potential is tremendous.

POWELL ON THE POTOMAC

by
Jeanne V. Bell

When it comes to Colin Powell, inside-the-beltway pundits have several traits in common: everyone has an opinion, but—except for journalists whose job it is was, certain politicians who have a vested interest in voicing their views, and a very few daring souls—practically no one is willing to talk on the record. Whether it is a matter of protecting their jobs or job options, not wanting to risk being wrong, or a reluctance to take sides until the lines were drawn, despite the heavy news coverage of Powell and "Will He or Won't He Run?," there was almost a conspiracy of silence among the power players when it came to stating where they stood, much less projecting the outcome.

A prominent publisher who also has worked in government and has held a high-level Presidential appointment said, "Colin Powell is the only general I know of—and that includes former Presidents—who is fully capable of being President of the United States." He added, "If he runs, he'll win. And he'll do a great job."

Another member of the Washington establishment said, "He would do better to hold back and wait until Dole is nominated and asks him to be on his ticket as Vice President." When, in response to that suggestion, a fellow insider asked, "What about Roger Wilkins' statement, 'It would be an act of self-diminution for Powell to accept that slot?' " The reply was, "That's what Lyndon Johnson said, and he was a helluva lot more stubborn and egotistical than Colin Powell, but when Jack Kennedy asked him to run, Lyndon accepted in a heartbeat."

Washington-based syndicated columnist Karen Feld was told by Powell insiders that his friends have been warning him not to believe his own press clippings and to be aware that if he were to announce he was a candidate, he immediately would become fair game for the media. "But Powell cannot be naive," she says. "He surrounds himself with highly-respected political strategists. Kenneth Duberstein, Powell's neighbor in McLean, Virginia, who was George Bush's White House Chief of Staff, is probably Powell's closest friend and advisor. Dick Armitage, another close friend, was Assistant Secretary of Defense when Powell was Chairman of the Joint Chiefs, and Powell is also very friendly with Senator Sam Nunn, a veteran Democrat who understands Washington and the electorate as well as anyone."

The word around Washington is that Powell was the only potential candidate who was of serious concern to both the leading Republican contender and the White House. But as for his running as anything other than a Democrat or Republican, the widespread consensus was that if he ran as an independent, he wouldn't have been able to raise enough money, and that if even if he could, at best he would only divide the Republican vote, so Clinton—who has been busy positioning himself as a moderate—would be guaranteed to win. But, some smart money says, if he runs with Dole, he'll carry the ticket. Still, many veteran election watchers noted that while we know Powell the hero, we don't know Powell the candidate, and, they pointed out, we must wait and see how he will hold up under public scrutiny. And the extent to which he will cause voters to cross party lines.

When the chips are down, there is considerable cohesiveness in the black community, but there is far from 100% agreement. There are those among the blacks who feel that they should stick together, but others resent the suggestion that African-Americans vote strictly along color lines. At the same time, as one political observer pointed out, the majority of African-American voters have traditionally registered as Democrats, so if Colin Powell runs as a Republican and attracts a large percentage of black voters, there will be a dramatic change in party registration.

Maudine R. Cooper, President of the Washington Urban League, was one of the few insiders willing to talk on the record. She said, "Without knowing his specific position on a number of issues, it's difficult to reach definitive conclusions about Colin Powell. However, there are three basic considerations on which any candidate for President must be judged. Is he or she an extremely able and honorable person? Is he or she fully qualified to be the President of the United States? Does he or she have the intelligence, ability, and experience to govern and make the difficult decisions with wisdom and resolve? The answer is Yes, Colin Powell qualifies in each of those categories."

She continued, "Americans, and especially African-Americans, are in desperate need of a hero, and Colin Powell fills that role admirably in every respect. But no one is perfect, so it's possible that when the media and Powell's opponents start digging, they might find some hidden flaws. But even if he were perfect in every respect, could Colin Powell get elected? "I think probably not."

Cooper added, "It seems reasonable to assume

that he would have the votes of many or most African-Americans. And many whites would be behind him 100%. But, we inside the beltway tend to underestimate the depth and breadth of racism in this country. So the big question is, when it is time to mark their ballots, will the majority cast their votes for the best candidate, or will we see the less-enlightened segment of the American population vote their prejudices and prevail? "I can only hope not."

From a different perspective, a very prominent, nationally known and respected black lawyer says, "I don't feel that I really know Colin Powell or his positions on any of the critical issues that will face this country. The fact that he reached the top in the military and understands the military complex does not necessarily mean that he understands the other needs of this country.

"I do not believe that color should be the basis on which we select our next president. George Washington, the military man, may have been ideal in his day, but there came the time when we needed Thomas Jefferson, the intellectual. What we must have now is a leader with a keen sensitivity to the wide range of problems and needs of this country and the many countries with which we must interact—a man with vision, both national and global."

Another African-American attorney, Koteles Alexander, managing partner of Alexander, Aponte & Marks, one of the largest multi-cultural, multi-ethnic law firms in the US, said, "I think the election of Colin Powell as President, particularly as the Republican party's candidate would be a powerful expression of the American ideal and citizenship. And I think he has a 50–50 chance of getting elected."

Caspar Weinberger, the Secretary of Defense under whom Powell served and also a neighbor of Powell's, said in an interview, "Quite a few people have talked to me about whether America is ready to accept a black candidate. I don't think that would be a factor at all. . . . With Colin, I never think of whether he's black or white or anything else."

Weinberger and many African-Americans have that trait in common. A recent *U.S. News* poll showed Powell receiving favorable ratings from 73% of whites, but only from 57% of blacks. The article continued, "To many Powell may be more of a name than a face; almost a fifth of those African-Americans who said they knew of Powell reported that they didn't know what race he was."

Everyone in Washington is a bit of a chameleon and there are times when politicians of all persuasions seem to blend into a unified whole. But the styles of Jesse Jackson and Colin Powell are totally opposite. Jackson is The Reverend and speaks and acts accordingly. Although he can be a quiet and persuasive speaker, most often he gives the impression that a prayer and/or a sermon will be forthcoming at any time. Jackson is not a Powell booster. He makes it clear that he doesn't know what Powell stands for and he doesn't trust the motives of those who support Powell.

Powell has the dignity of the archetypal general, but those who know him well describe him as soft-spoken but authoritative, and always a man of reason. His supporters were—still are—confident that he is capable of running the affairs of this country, both at home and abroad, far more ably than any candidate on the horizon. His most ardent detractors are found at the far right. The fact that he has indicated that he is pro-choice was all the evidence they seem to need that his positions on all or most other matters will be antithetical to them.

Writing in *The Washington Post*, veteran journalist Charles Krauthammer, a contributing editor of the very conservative *Weekly Standard*, put it this way: "In an ironic and tragic turn of the civil rights revolution, there is today a powerful movement within the black community away from Martin Luther King, Jr.'s vision of integration toward a new kind of separatism, self-imposed and adversarial. Its most extreme advocate is, of course,

Louis Farrakhan, who portrays African-Americans as an occupied people in an alien land.

"Against this tragic turn toward black separatism comes Colin Powell, a man who calls his autobiography not a personal journey, not an African American journey, but "An American Journey"; whose self identity is one of soldier, patriot and, above all, American; who, while declaring himself to be proudly American, at the same time declares himself not just incidentally black but proudly black.

"This deliberate, self-possessed merging of two identities offers by deed and example an extremely powerful alternative to Farrakhan-like separatism."

In a Letter to the Editor of *The Washington Post*, Milton Eisenberg, a partner in the prestigious Washington law firm of Fried, Frank, Harris, Shriver & Jacobson, wrote, "I was in complete disagreement with Charles Krauthammer . . ." But it was not about Krauthammer's evaluation of Powell's viability as a candidate or as an effective president, but rather about the reasoning behind it. Eisenberg stressed that Powell's presidency would not guarantee an end to racial problems, but that he would be "a President for all Americans." He concluded, "I believe Colin Powell's candidacy should be judged on his merits and not on his race. He has the stature, the character, the integrity, and the experience to serve as a great president. That's why he deserves Mr. Krauthammer's and every other American's serious consideration."

But Pat Buchanan, appearing on ABC's "This Week with David Brinkley," warned of a full-scale revolt by Christian conservatives if Powell were to win the nominations and tilt the party toward a pro-choice position on abortion.

"You'd have Christian Coalition folks breaking loose, you'd have people walking out of the convention if Colin Powell tries to impose his agenda," said Buchanan, who is himself making a second try for the GOP nomination. Buchanan said he would not support an end to the party's pro-life, anti-gun control and anti-affirmative action positions, but stopped short of saying that he would leave the party.

At least one leading Republican disagreed with Buchanan. Although he took pains to go on record that he will not publicly endorse any candidate, the word went around that among his friends, former President Bush spoke enthusiastically about Powell.

Local civic leader Kerry H. Stowell, who heads SoSound Productions and serves on the Board of Directors of the DC League of Republican Women, said, "Powell seems to have created a groundswell of enthusiasm, not so much for what he has said but for what he has not said." Stowell remarked that his book tour was an almost unprecedented success, but the analysts seemed to be divided on whether it was a matter of curiosity about the man or an interest in what might have been gleaned about him as a presidential candidate by reading between the lines of what he had written. However," she adds, "the number of Powell's books that were sold may far exceed the number of people who actually read it. But that may be another indicator of popularity rather than an indication of a lack of interest."

Stowell continued, "Was he being looked at as a black man? Not really. The politically savvy are not interested in his color, only in his viability as a candidate. As for the talk that he might run as an independent, that's exactly what it is—talk. It is doubtful that he would ever have had a chance to succeed as an independent. Even if he could have raised the money, which may have been remotely possible earlier but would be extremely difficult at this late date, he didn't have a political team in place, and to build an effective organization from the ground up takes years."

Stowell points out that he has distanced himself from Jesse Jackson and he stayed away from Louis Farrakhan and the Million's Man March. Would the black political activists with whom she often come-in contact support Powell? Stowell thinks

"They were waiting to see him define his platform. But at this point, I do not believe they saw him as the candidate of a black constituency." What about her neighbors at the exclusive Watergate apartments? Stowell says that among her neighbors, the majority of whom are Republicans, "With the notable exception of Bob and Elizabeth Dole, who are also Watergate dwellers, there does not seem to be any overwhelming commitment to a specific candidate. Everyone is in a wait-and-see mood. But," she says, "there are quite a few military people to whom I have spoken . . . who are still offended at Powell's public criticism of President Bush while serving in the military. They believe that he was out of order . . . making public statements about his Commander in Chief."

There were two principal Powell-support organizations at work: The Exploratory Draft Powell for President Committee, a grass roots group of about 3000 which has generated and distributed tens of thousands of buttons and bumper stickers that are circulated in major cities and the early primary states; Citizens for Colin Powell, which numbered about 3,000, headed by Chuck Kelly, Tex McCrary, and Stephen Ambrose. Kelly and McCrary were active in the Draft Eisenhower movement and Ambrose is author of a major Eisenhower biography. Their primary focus on identifying potential funding sources in the event that Powell declared himself a candidate.

John Topping, Jr., a somewhat-establishment Washington, DC, attorney who has been involved in civic and political activities, both nationally and locally, and became Chairman of the Lawyers Coordinating Committee of the Exploratory Draft Powell for President Committee, explained, "I had been looking for a candidate with a vision and a willingness to look ahead. Someone who would focus on moving toward solving the problems we'll be facing in the next century. Upon checking," he said, "I found that in this notoriously cynical, back-biting city filled with negative feelings about virtually everything and everyone, Colin Powell was the rare anomaly. He was respected, admired, and liked. I spoke with dozens of people who had known and worked with him, people at every level—his seniors, his peers, and his juniors—and, without exception, they described him as 'a straight shooter, great to work with, and always moving toward constructive ends.'

"I became involved in the national Draft-Powell effort because I was convinced that although he comes from the military, he has a remarkable ability to lead his countrymen, not just his troops. As I learned more about him, I became convinced that as a leader, Colin Powell belongs with Abraham Lincoln and Theodore Roosevelt. He is uniquely able to summon this country to greatness and, I think, he will someday be placed among the great men on Mount Rushmore."

Mel Burton, Political Strategist and Consultant to the Exploratory Draft Colin Powell for President Committee, declared:

"I support General Powell because of his character, integrity, and leadership ability, and because of the positions he has held as National Security Advisor to the President and as Chairman of the Joint Chiefs of Staff. These positions enabled him to have discussions with the President concerning national and international affairs, from which he gained great insights into the problems confronting America today. General Powell is not awed by power because he has had experience wielding power.

"The General, perhaps second to Nelson Mandela, is the most widely known and respected person in international affairs.

"The General is respected by the sovereigns of all the world's nations and states.

"General Powell is needed to set this country on the proper course for healing the discord which has arisen between the various groups of citizens."

Georgetown resident and community activist Barbara Zartman describes herself as ". . . the kind of Republican who cut her political teeth in the days of Nelson Rockefeller and New York Senator

Jack Javits." But, she explains, her criminal studies of the riots of the 60's—and the big government programs they spawned—left her with a deep distrust of answers from Washington. Zartman, Deputy Director of the Peace Corps during the Bush Administration, notes the irony that "At the very time centralized governments are failing around the globe, many Beltway liberals still fight the impulse to trust local communities to find local solutions."

Zartman says she first opposed the idea of Powell's candidacy, ". . . fearing that the mad-dog nature of so much current political commentary could destroy a national treasure: a man who rose above race—and race-hatred—to lead the greatest military force in the world." She cautioned, "This is capital that should not be spent nonchalantly. He could head a Ford Foundation or a similar charitable institution and make tremendous impact on the problems that have plagued us for much too long—and the new ones we are still seeking to define."

Powell's ability to mute conservative voices convinced Zartman that he could overcome the opposition of the more zealous Republican right. She was confident that could also bring back to the Republican tent (larger than the Buchanan team seems to wish) large numbers of more moderate women who have felt they were invited out of the party in the last dozen years. "Colin Powell has the ability to challenge us to be tolerant, not because we are compromisers, but because we seek to understand one another," said Zartman. "He acknowledges there are problems in American society, but quietly reminds us, 'They are ours to fix.' "

Roderick Gaines, vice-president for Business and Community Development of First Interstate Bank of California, a vice-president of TWA during his 12 years in Washington and still a frequent visitor to DC and an unofficial member of several inner circles, said he hopes Powell will support affirmative action to at least some extent. Gaines confided that without it, he might not have been hired for his first corporate job. He stressed, however, that while affirmative action opened the door for him, it was performance that enabled him to stay in the job and work his way up the corporate ladder. He spoke of Powell as a "positive enigma," and said that even though Powell has not spelled out his position, " . . . there are good reasons to believe that he would not be operating from a black perspective, but would endeavor to ensure that all policies would be fair—that he would not be skewed toward helping African-Americans, but would treat everybody the same." He added that he was confident of his assumption that Powell would be "reasonable, fair, and logical, and would provide an excellent model of how a President should function." He added, "In this era of moral decay, our country needs a President who will be demonstrably honorable and ethical, both in his official role and as a loyal husband and good father to his children."

Sarah McClendon, White House and Pentagon correspondent, in her 86th year, but still able to dip her pen in acid, conducted her own fact-finding expedition on Colin Powell. Below are some of her conclusions.

"He has points in his favor: good-looking, friendly, good book revealing some things we all ought to know, would be an easy transition from highest black in Defense to highest office—Presidency. (Many black generals in Army now.)

Facts against him:

"He was pushed rapidly up the ladder by former President George Bush, former Defense Secretary Frank Carlucci, and former Assistant Secretary of Defense Richard Armitage. Their agenda would continue—lots of wars, most of the budget going to weapons of death, many untested, billions of dollars worth of weapons undervalued, sold or given away around the world to our enemies and our friends, to foment wars but also to make profits for sellers with profits not going back to Treasury but into their Swiss bank accounts. Under him, CIA would continue to run the country.

"Powell allowed multi billions of dollars of these weapons which had been paid for by taxpayers to go overseas. They fomented more wars. Powell often failed to give military advice if contrary to stated desires of his superior warlords. Maybe one does not defy a President, Vice-president, or top general.

"Powell is accused of covering up US slaughter of a village in Vietnam. He failed to send to US troops in Somalia a certain kind of fighting aircraft. Our soldiers were attacked and could not defend themselves. Eighteen died and over 70 were wounded, their bodies mutilated and drawn through the streets for natives to see.

"Powell is certainly not an Eisenhower. Attempt by public relations man in NY, Tex McCrary, to compare him with Ike is shameful. But like Ike, Powell only knows the military. He would be no good for solving vast majority of problems across the nation.

"I am told he received over $6.5 million in advance for book and that the various media have spent $3 million blowing him up. But it now looks as if he will get to the White House, largely on the backs of Republicans and certain left-wing liberal Democrats in Congress who want Clinton out. Powell will be picked over Dole, who deserves it. Gore and Nunn as Democratic ticket cannot win. Powell gets it."

Sarah's friends and fans are hoping that she will soon outgrow her shyness and be able to say and write what she really thinks.

Another senior correspondent, Helen Thomas, White House Bureau Chief for UPI, also known for her candor, has a different view. She says, "Colin Powell is respected both as a general and as a person. In fact, people seem to put him on a pedestal. And he is demonstrably able. However, he would probably need to bone up on domestic affairs—an area that is of great concern to our country at this time.

"His overwhelmingly successful book tour must have been a heavy experience and may have made him more inclined to run. And he certainly has a great opportunity, if that is what he decides to do.

"His views are more liberal than the conservative right which seems to control the Republican party. He may be modifying them to some extent. But even now some very distinguished and influential leaders on the right are definitely supporting him. He is a formidable and seemingly very admirable person."

The head of a conservative Washington think tank put it this way: "He has a good reputation and has never been involved in anything unsavory. He has the qualities of leadership. If he put together an effective team, he would be both a capable President and a unifying factor might be able to mend the cleavages among diverse minorities.

Pulitzer prize-winning journalist Jack Nelson, who has been with the Washington Bureau of the *Los Angeles Times* for 26 years, 21 of them as Bureau Chief, noted that some of Powell's friends and advisers were indicating that it was becoming more likely that he would seek the Republican presidential nomination. Nelson heard "that Powell has been consulting with a wide range of political gurus and looking at possible campaign strategies." He had been told that the fact that Dole seems to be dropping in the polls may added to the likelihood of a Powell candidacy. But, Nelson said, "As nearly as I can ascertain, Powell has not disclosed his intentions to even his closest associates."

Chairman of then-President George Bush's re-election campaign Robert N. Teeter told Nelson, "There are a lot of signs he's leaning toward running. . . . The question is whether he can win the Republican nomination. And the answer is, he can. . . . That's not saying he would," Teeter continued, "but if he got nominated, he would be elected."

Nelson's list of others who have conferred with Powell includes Marlin Fitzwater, White House press secretary for Presidents Reagan and Bush; William Kristol, who was Vice-President Quayle's chief of staff; former Education Secretary William J. Bennett; and former Secretary of Housing and Urban Development Jack Kemp. Also among Powell's friends and advisers is former President Carter. Nelson says that during a meeting in Atlanta where Powell finished the last leg of his book tour, General Powell and the former President met for about an hour. Carter declined to comment on their conversation, but a longtime associate of the former President quoted Carter as saying that Powell left him with "the distinct impression" that he is planning to run for the GOP nomination. Nelson understood that Powell asked Carter numerous questions about his experiences with campaigning and fundraising.

Although Powell remained resolute about not indicating his intentions, he is reported to have canceled a college speaking engagement with an explanation to the school's president that he needed time to consider "the most momentous decision of my life."

Nelson heard that although some of Powell's friends said they believed that the overwhelming reception he received on his month-long, 27-city tour to promote his best-selling book may have pointed him toward making the race, Powell reportedly told some associates that his decision was more difficult at the end of the tour than before he began it. And Powell was quoted as saying that his many consultations had given him a better understanding of the complexities and challenges of mounting a campaign.

Nelson points out that the entry of Powell, a former Chairman of the Joint Chiefs of Staff and the first African-American in history that polls have indicated would have a serious chance at winning the presidency, would drastically alter the playing field for the 1996 campaign.

A key Dole supporter, former Senator Warren B. Rudman, a Republican from New Hampshire, said that while Powell would be a formidable candidate, Dole is "very well organized in all the cities, towns and precincts. I still don't think he'll get in, but it would be a major impact and a two-man race for the nomination if he does," Rudman said.

According to former Secretary Bennett, "There's a conservative establishment . . . which is frankly going bonkers right now, because the grass roots, the individuals, people who actually vote, like Colin Powell."

A CBS–*New York Times* poll released at the end of October found that if Powell entered, he would cut deeply into Dole's support and could become the immediate front runner.

Subsequent polls showed Powell with greater strength than President Clinton or Senate Majority Leader Dole. Fitzwater and other sources said the fact that Dole had been consistently running behind Clinton in recent preference polls while Powell ran ahead of the President in most of them has put pressure on Powell to enter the race.

As interest in Powell's possible candidacy grew, Dole seemingly tried to ignored it. He did, however, note that he was not perturbed about the prospect of Powell's candidacy. "In politics you have two days when you're very popular—the day before you get in and the day you get out," he said. "He isn't in yet."

It was clear that Powell's maneuvering and the senator's slippage in the polls caused Dole's campaign, as well as Clinton's, to take notice and reconsider strategy.

A Dole campaign advisor, who asked not to be identified, said: "I've been totally convinced for some time that Powell is coming into the race as a Republican and it's going to have an impact on raising money and everything else." He added, "I don't know whether the senator believes he's coming in or not."

A senior Clinton aide said that in drawing up a strategic plan, the President's campaign assumed it should prepare for a run against the best possible Republican candidate. The aide added: "A race with Powell in it would be a lot tighter because he would be a candidate with more pluses than minuses.

"We've been hearing from some people who are

convinced Powell's going to run," the aide said, "but we don't obsess about it."

There is one person who probably did obsess about it, and that person will be a significant factor in Powell's decision and future plans. Alma Powell is widely viewed as a substantial political asset. She comes from a distinguished family that has been part of the black aristocracy for several generations. She has an understated sense of cultural security and social confidence: she fits into society, black and white. She is also at home with power—her own and others'. Discussing what kind of First Lady she would be, Caspar Weinberger compared her to Barbara Bush, saying, "She is a lady who is comfortable with herself and therefore makes everybody feel very much at ease." He added that people around the world feel the same way about her and that she would be a genuine asset in the White House.

Alma Powell made it clear that although she would support a decision to run, she personally does not favor it. A prominent woman who is a close friend of hers confided that she had said, "Alma, if Colin runs, we will put everything at our disposal behind you. And for our country's sake, I hope he does. For your sake, I hope he doesn't."

The possible candidate's wife said, "I was looking forward to our quiet times together. If he runs, we won't have any. But that's the least of it. Every

President in recent years has been in constant danger. That would be magnified many times for Colin."

When, following his announcement that he would not run, Powell was asked about reports that his wife suffered from depression, he said, "My wife has depression. She has had it for many years. It is not a family secret. It is easily controlled with proper medication." Her experience, he added, should prompt others with that problem to seek medical help. On the same subject, one of Alma Powell's close friends said, "I've known her for years and been with her often; I've never seen her other than upbeat and energetic. So she's living proof that the right medications really are effective."

As time passed, there were many indicators that Powell might run. The polls were encouraging and his supporters grew in numbers and enthusiasm. When it was indicated that he would be reaching his decision before Thanksgiving, Washington was buzzing with speculation. It seemed that the number of insiders who were certain that he would run slightly exceeded the number who were equally certain that he would not.

Among the media mighty who predicted that Powell would run were ABC correspondent Sam Donaldson, John McLaughlin, Tim Russert, Rush Limbaugh, Jack Germond, David Broder, Morton

Kondracke, Ben Wattenberg, Carl Rowan, Charles Krauthammer, and Evan Thomas. David Brinkley, Fred Barnes and Eleanor Clift were among the few who said he would not. When Powell announced that he would not run, Sam Donaldson said, "I been wrong before. What happens to a lot of us is we transfer to believing that what we want to happen is going to happen, rather than being objective."

Jack Germond made another point. He said, "If we were right all the time, they couldn't afford to pay our salaries."

A number of leading political strategists virtually bet their reputations that Powell would run and win. They included William Kristol, William Bennett and other high-profile Washington insiders.

On November 8, as the speculation seemed to be reaching a feverish pitch, in a statement to the media and the people of the United States, Retired General Colin Luther Powell said, "To offer myself as a candidate for President requires . . . the kind of passion and the kind of commitment that I felt every day of my 35 years as a soldier . . . a calling that I do not yet hear. And therefore, I cannot go forward. I will not be a candidate for President or any other elective office in 1996."

Powell also flatly rejected a possible nomination for Vice president. "I have ruled it out," he said. Although he emphasized that he will seek no political office in 1996, he did not rule himself out of political competition for all time.

For now, he explained, "I will remain in private life and seek other ways to serve. I have a deep love for this country . . . I will find other ways to contribute to the important work needed to keep us moving forward.

"I will continue to speak out forcefully in the future on the issues of the day, as I have been doing in recent weeks. I will do so as a member of the Republican Party and try to assist the party in broadening its appeal. I believe I can help the party of Lincoln move once again close to the spirit of Lincoln. I will also try to find ways for me to help heal the racial divide that still exists within our society."

The concluding words of his formal remarks were, "How honored I am that so many of you found me worthy of your support. It says more about America than it says about me. In one generation we have moved from denying a black man service at the lunch counter to elevating one to the highest military office in the nation and to being a serious contender for the presidency. This is a magnificent country. I am proud to be one of its sons."

Before announcing his decision, Powell said, "The welfare of my family had to be uppermost in my mind." He added, "Ultimately, however, I had to look deep into my own soul . . ."

During the questions from the media that followed the announcement, Mrs. Powell stated clearly that although she had expressed concerns, they were not a deciding factor in her husband's decision. However, someone close to the picture said that two nights before the announcement Ken Duberstein and Dick Armitage had been at the Powell's house for a long meeting and Alma Powell was very explicit that she was not in favor of her husband becoming a candidate.

While declaring that he would not be a contestant in the next campaign, Powell did not rule himself out of political competition forever. "The future is the future," he said. And already there is talk of him as Secretary of State and other top positions.

Following Powell's announcement that he would not run, a Clinton aide said, "We've dodged a big bullet." But have they? Or might General Powell follow in the steps of another general who captured the hearts and minds of the American public? In 1953, after repeatedly declaring that he would neither run nor be drafted for the office, General Dwight D. Eisenhower became the 34th President of the United States.

(Numerologists may be interested to note that in 1953 Dwight Eisenhower was inaugurated as the

34th President of the United States. If Bill Clinton is not reelected, in 1996, 43 years later, the 43rd President of the United States will be elected.)

Probably typical of Powell's organized supporters, lawyer John Topping, who had been in the trenches working for Powell, said, "After the most masterful declination in political history, it's very conceivable that if General Powell feels that he is in a position to be effective, he will agree to run four years from now. And it's probable that this time he would start earlier. Our organization will become dormant, but we will be certainly be watching him and we will stay in touch."

A person wise in the ways of Washington said, "The important question is, 'What will Powell be doing for the next two- to four-years? Is he a political animal? If so, he can have a real impact on the policies of this country. If he makes his voice heard, both parties will be looking over their shoulders to gage his activities and opinions. He could also have a tremendous impact in the private sector. It is really up to him.

"Another possibility is that he will become an elder statesman—better still, an ombudsman for the American people, a role that this country needs as never before.

"It's still a mystery. We've been hearing from political analysts about a man who has never been political. It's possible that we should have been hearing from psychologists, behaviorists or others who are knowledgeable about the human psyche."

An old Washington hand who knows history, Washington, politics and Powell said, "Of all the U.S. Presidents, only three have really connected with the people: Abraham Lincoln, Franklin Delano Roosevelt and John F. Kennedy. Colin Powell would have been the fourth. Maybe he still will be."

So, once again, Washington will play the wait-and-see game. While there is sure to be ongoing speculation about whether he has other plans for his political future, many reasonable people will assume that Colin Powell's decision was—and his future decisions will be—based on the same considerations that have been his guiding principals for as long as anyone can remember: Service to his country and concern for his family.

COLIN POWELL TIMELINE

April 1937
: Colin Luther Powell born in Harlem

1942
: Powell family moves from Harlem to South Bronx

1954
: Powell graduates from Morris High School; enters CCNY

Fall 1954
: Powell enrolls in ROTC

June 1958
: Distinguished Military Graduate Powell enters basic training at Ft. Benning, GA

Summer 1961
: Powell's first three years' enlistment is up; he re-enlists

August 1962
: Powell marries Alma Johnson

December 1962
Powell arrives in Saigon

March 1963
Son Michael Kevin Powell is born

November 1963
Powell returns to US

August 1964
Powell begins Infantry Officers Advanced Course, designed to prepare infantry captains to take over command of a company

April 1965
Daughter Linda Powell is born

July 1968
Powell returns for second tour of Vietnam

June 1969
Powell is accepted for fall class in School of Government and Business Administration at George Washington University

July 1969
Powell returns to the States

May 1970
Daughter Annemarie Powell is born

May 1971
Powell receives MBA from George Washington University

December 1971
Powell selected by the President's Commission

to serve as a 1972–73 White House Fellow at the Office of Management and Budget (OMB)

January 1973
: White House Fellows travel to the Soviet Union

June 1973
: White House Fellows travel to China, then Powell goes to Korea

September 1974
: Powell returns from Korea to work at the Pentagon

August 1975
: Powell begins classes at National War College at Fort McNair, Washington, DC

February 1976
: Powell receives accelerated promotion to full Colonel, assumes command of 2nd Brigade, I0Ist Ariborne, Fort Campbell, KY, following war college

February 1977
: New career opportunities with Brzezinski and Kester. Powell chooses Kester

April 1978
: Luther Theophilus Powell, Colin's father, dies

December 1978
: Powell promoted to brigadier general

1987
: Operation Just Cause in Panama

1981

Powell assigned to Fort Carson, CO

1982

Powell becomes deputy commander general, US Army Combined Arms Combat Development Activity, Fort Leavenworth, KS

June 1983

Powell becomes senior military advisor to Secretary of Defense Caspar Weinberger.

October 1983

US invasion of Grenada

June 1984

Maud Ariel Powell, Colin's mother, dies

1986

US raid on Libya

July 1986

Powell takes over US Army V Corps in Frankfurt, West Germany

December, 1986

Powell returns to Washington to work for Frank Carlucci in National Security

November 1987

President Reagan promotes Powell to National Security Advisor

January 1989

President Bush relieves Powell of White House duties in favor of his own National Security Advisor

---

April 1989

Powell receives fourth star and takes over US Forces Command

August 1989

Powell offered chairmanship of Joint Chiefs of Staff

December 1989

US invades Panama and ousts Noriega

January 17–February 28, 1991

Persian Gulf War

September 1993

Powell retires from the military

September 1995

Publication of *My American Journey*

November 8, 1995

Powell announces he will not run for political office in 1996

SELECTED BIBLIOGRAPHY

Adler, Bill. *The Generals: The New American Heroes*. New York: Avon Books, 1991.

Adler, Jerry. "The Final Push." *Newsweek*, Special Issue (Spring/Summer 1991): 99.

Apple, R. W. Jr. "A Coveted General Rides Toward '96 Without a Banner." *The New York Times*. (September 25, 1994): Sec. 1.

Associated Press. "Excerpts from the Pentagon Briefing." *The New York Times* (Dec. 21, 1989) Sec. A.

Auster, Bruce B. "In the Footsteps of Two Georges." *U.S. News & World Report* (Feb. 4, 1991): 26–27.

Binder, James L. "Gen. Colin L. Powell." *Army*, Apr. 1990: 22ff.

Binkin, Martin, and Mark J. Eitelberg. *Blacks in the Military*. Washington, DC: Brookings Institution, 1982.

Blue, Rose, and Corinne J. Nadeau. *Colin Powell: Straight to the Top*. Brookfield, CT: The Millbrook Press, 1991.

Booker, Simeon. "Black General at the Summit of U.S. Power," *Ebony* (July, 1988): 146ff.

Brown, Warren. *Colin Powell*. New York: Chelsea House, 1992.

Bunch, Bryan and Alexander Hellemans. *The Timetables of Technology*. Touchstone, 1994.

Campbell, Joseph. *The Hero with a Thousand Faces.* The Bollingen Foundation, 1949.

Church, George J. "Marching to a Conclusion: The Night that Bush Decided." *Time* (Mar. 4, 1991): 18–25.

Crowley, Kiernan. "Powell Gung-Ho for Drug Tests." *The New York Post* (Apr. 17, 1991).

Dalfiume, Richard M. *Desegregation of the United States Armed Forces: Fighting on Two Fronts, 1939–1952.* Columbia: University of Missouri Press, 1969.

Davis, Benjamin O., Jr. *Benjamin O. Davis, Jr., American: An Autobiography.* Washington, DC: Smithsonian Institution, 1991.

Devroy, Ann, and George C. Wilson. "Bush Picks 'Complete Soldier' Powell to Head the Joint Chiefs." *The Washington Post* (Aug. 11, 1989): Sec. A.

Fletcher, Marvin E. *America's First Black General.* Lawrence: University of Kansas, 1989.

Fowler, Arlen. *The Black Infantry in the West, 1869–1891.* Westport, CT: Greenwood Press, 1971.

Friedman, Saul. "Four-Star Warrior." *Long Island Newsday Magazine.* (Feb. 11, 1990): 10ff.

Frisby, Michael K. "Colin Powell: At the Top But Mindful of His Roots." *The Boston Sunday Globe* (Apr. 21, 1991): Sec. A.

"Gen. Colin Powell's Advice to Young Blacks Today: Prepare and Be Ready." *Jet* (Sept. 11, 1989): 12ff.

Gordon, Michael R. and Bernard E. Trainor. "Beltway Warrior." *The New York Times* (August 27, 1995): Sec. 6.

Gordon, Michael R. "Top Soviet General Tells U.S. Not to Attack in Gulf." *The New York Times* (Oct. 3, 1990): Sec. A.

Greider, William. "Colin-Izing America." *Rolling Stone* (Nov. 16, 1995): 45.

Grun, Bernard. *The Timetables of History*. New York: Simon and Schuster, 1975, 1979.

Hampson, Rick. "The General's Bloc: Tracing Gen. Powell's Roots." New York: The Associated Press, Feb. 9, 1991.

Healy, Melissa. "Powell Honors Blacks Who Served." *The Los Angeles Times* (Aug. 18, 1989) Sec. A.

Ifill, Gwen. "Armed Forces Making Strides, Powell Says." *The Washington Post* (Aug. 18, 1989): A11ff.

Jackson, Derrick Z. "Powell in '96?" *The Boston Globe* (Feb. 3, 1991): Op-Ed.

Leckie, William H. *The Buffalo Soldiers: A Narrative of the Negro Cavalry in the West*. Norman: University of Oklahoma Press, 1985.

Macintyre, Ben. "Left right Left right." Times Newspapers Limited. (August 26, 1995).

Motley, Mary. *The Invisible Soldiers: The Experience of the Black Soldier, World War II*. Detroit: Wayne State University Press, 1987.

Ottley, Roi, and William J. Weatherby, eds. *The Negro in New York: An Informal Social History*. New York: The New York Public Library, 1967.

Potts, Paula Lee. "A Conversation with Alma Powell." *Military Lifestyle* (May 1990): 38ff.

Powell, Colin. With Joseph E. Persico. *My American Journey*. New York: Random House, 1995.

Powell, Colin L. "From CCNY to the White House," *The Public Interest 94* (Winter 1989) 87ff.

Prados, John. Keeper of the Keys: *A History of the National Security Council from Truman to Bush*. New York: Morrow, 1991.

Quarles, Benjamin. *The Negro in the Making of America*.

2nd rev. ed. New York: Collier Macmillan Publishers, 1987.

Rennert, Richard. Editor. *Book of Firsts: Leaders of America*. New York: Chelsea House, 1994.

Reuters. "Powell Links His Rise to All Black Soldiers." *The New York Times* (Aug. 10, 1991): Sec. A.

Rowan, Carl T. "Called To Service: The Colin Powell Story." *Reader's Digest* (Dec. 1989): 121ff.

Senna, Carl. *Colin Powell: A Man of War and Peace*. New York: Walker, 1994

Smith, Graham. *When Jim Crow Met John Bull: Black American Soldiers in World War II in Britain*. New York: St. Martin's Press, 1988.

Weinberger, Caspar W. "General Powell—an Inside View." *Forbes* (Jan. 22, 1990): 31.

Wilson, George C. "Gen. Powell Due to Lead Joint Chiefs." *The Washington Post* (Aug. 10, 1989): 1ff.

Woodward, Bob. *The Commanders*. New York: Simon and Schuster, 1991.